ROYAL RESIDENCES

ROYAL RESIDENCES

JOHN MARTIN ROBINSON

MACDONALD & CO
LONDON & SYDNEY

First published in Great Britain in 1982 by
Macdonald & Co (Publishers) Ltd

Maxwell House
74 Worship Street, London EC2A 2EN

ISBN 0 356 07908 2

Printed in Great Britain in 1982 by
Hazell Watson & Viney Ltd
Aylesbury, Bucks

CONTENTS

ACKNOWLEDGEMENTS

I am grateful to the following for help in assembling the illustrations: Sir Geoffrey Shakerley who has taken a number of photographs specially for this book, including those in colour; Mr Stephen Croad of the National Monument Record (England); Miss Kitty Croft of the National Monuments Record (Scotland); Mr John Phillips of the Greater London Record Office; Hon. Mrs Hugh Roberts of the Royal Library Windsor and Mr Jon Whiteley of the Ashmolean Museum, Oxford. Mr Marcus Bishop of the Lord Chamberlain's Office.

John Martin Robinson

PLANS

ILLUSTRATIONS

BLACK AND WHITE

COLOUR

SOURCES

The following illustrations are reproduced by gracious permission of Her Majesty The Queen: pp. 85, 86, 87, 132, 133 (bottom), 185 (right). Colour photographs: 13, 14, 18, 23, 25.

The author and publishers wish to acknowledge the following, for permission to reproduce other illustrations:

R. J. Berkeley, Berkeley Castle: pp. 39 (top), 57 (top), 90 (top).

Bodleian Library, Oxford: pp. 13 (bottom), 83.

British Museum: p. 11.

Country Life: pp. 14, 31 (bottom), 59, 124, 149, 155, 164, 165 (top right, and bottom), 166 (right), 188 (bottom), 189 (bottom).

Department of the Environment: Colour photograph: 7.

Greater London Council: pp. 29, 30, 38, 41, 42 (right, top and bottom), 43, 60, 68 (top), 71 (right, and bottom left), 75, 80, 91, 92/93, 94, 110, 111, 113, 115, 116, 119, 120, 121 (top right, and bottom), 126 (bottom), 129, 139, 140, 141, 143, 145, 146, 150, 151, 156, 157, 158, 159, 168, 189 (top). Colour photographs: 19, 20, 21.

A. F. Kersting: pp. 21, 66 (top), 73 (far right).

Eric de Maré: p. 117.

Museum of London: p. 49.

National Monuments Record: pp. 3, 4, 10 (bottom), 15 (top right, and bottom), 16 (bottom), 22 (right), 23, 24, 27, 31 (top), 34, 39 (bottom), 40, 44, 45, 46, 48, 53, 54, 55, 57 (bottom), 58, 61, 68 (bottom, right and left), 72, 73 (left), 76, 88, 89, 90 (bottom), 95, 96, 97, 98, 99, 101, 102, 103 (top), 104, 106, 109, 112, 117, 169, 171, 172, 173, 175, 176, 180, 181, 182, 184.

National Portrait Gallery, London, courtesy of: p. 42 (left).

Royal Commission on Ancient Monuments, Scotland: p. 179.

Royal Institute of British Architects: pp. 66 (bottom), 67, 69, 71 (top left), 73 (right), 82, 103 (bottom), 114, 125, 185 (left), 188 (top).

Walter Scott, Bradford: p. 16 (top).

Sir Geoffrey Shakerley: pp. 130, 163: Colour photographs: 2, 5, 6, 8, 9, 10, 11, 12, 15, 17, 16, 22.

Mrs Tunnicliffe: p. 144.

Dean and Canons of Windsor: p. 15 (top left).

Dean and Chapter of Westminster Abbey: Colour photograph: 3.

Westminster City Libraries: pp. 9, 10 (top, right and left), 20, 22 (top, and left).

Woodrow Wyatt: p. 166 (left).

— INTRODUCTION —

The purpose of this book is to trace the architectural history of the English royal residences from the Saxons up to the beginning of the twentieth century. There are many studies of individual palaces or groups of palaces, especially of those which still exist, but surprisingly few which cover the whole sweep, apart from the monumental *History of the King's Works* which is not yet completed and in any case is probably too detailed for the general reader. This wider treatment of the subject is worth attempting not just because the greatest architectural interest of the English royal residences lies in those buildings which have been destroyed, rather than in those which survive in use, but also because such a chronological survey has the additional interest of reflecting the development of the court and royal taste over the centuries. This book is intended to cover all the principal royal residences except castles, though some major fortified palaces like the Tower, Winchester and Windsor have been included as they are considered to have been, for at least part of their history, more important as residences than as centres of military power.

The English royal residences are of two basic kinds – state palaces intended for the occupation of the king together with the full court, and private houses or retreats intended by the monarch for retirement from the formality of court life. There are considerable differences of architecture and planning between these two types of houses. The latter are not all that different from the houses of any gentleman; the former on the other hand have a more ceremonial character with guards of honour, accommodation for courtiers, and a sequence of state rooms planned to regulate public access to the monarch. The line between these two categories of royal residence is not clearcut, and often a building which began as a private royal house has with the passage of time developed into a fully-fledged palace. St James's, for instance, was built by Henry VIII as a retreat from the court at Whitehall, but by the eighteenth century it had become the principal metropolitan palace of the Kings of England. Buckingham Palace was acquired by George III as a private house adjacent to St James's, but in its turn it has become the chief royal palace in London. The process is continuous and in the present reign can be seen overtaking Balmoral Castle. Balmoral was built by Queen Victoria and Prince Albert as the ultimate in private royal retreats, but is in the process of becoming an official royal residence in Scotland and now has uniformed sentries posted outside in place of Queen Victoria's single village policeman.

This seemingly inevitable trend towards greater formality is one of two conflicting forces which have determined the character of the royal residences. On the one hand, there is the striving after architectural grandeur in order to glorify the public setting of the king and the court. On the other, there is the wish for peace and quiet, intimacy and privacy on the part of the monarch himself. The extent to which one or other of these aspirations predominated in the architecture of a particular reign depended very much on the character of individual monarchs. George III, who disliked pomp and preferred quiet family life, put much effort into building relatively small private houses for himself and his consort. George IV, however, had a highly developed sense of the glory of kingship and spent his time extravagantly reconstructing the various royal residences to provide as much grandeur and dignity as possible in the ceremonial backdrops of his life. A chronological survey of the royal residences is a record of the architectural results of these contradictory objectives – grandeur and privacy. The continuous retreat of the monarch to new fastnesses is expressed in the development of ever longer sequences of state and private rooms, separate 'trianons' and private country houses. The unrelenting encroachment of the court, resulting in private rooms becoming state rooms and private houses of the king becoming state palaces, expresses the wish of his leading subjects to gain access to the person of the monarch, who for centuries was the source of power, honour and riches.

The architectural quality of the English royal residences reached its peak in the Middle Ages and early sixteenth century in the work of Henry II, Henry III, Edward III, Richard II, Henry V and Henry VIII. This is an appropriate reflection of the strength of the monarchy. The English medieval kings were the most powerful and politically sophisticated, though not the richest, in Europe. They held sway over a fluctuating hegemony wider than the kingdom of England itself. In France they were Dukes of Normandy and Aquitaine, Counts of Anjou, Maine and Touraine. In the British Isles they were Kings of England, Lords of Ireland, conquerors of Wales and would-be overlords of Scotland. The constitutional revolutions of the seventeenth century greatly reduced the personal power of the monarch, with the ironic result that the creation of a united Kingdom of England and Scotland and the development of a world-wide British Empire from the seventeenth century to the early twentieth century has only a muted reflection in the architecture of the palaces of its titular head. The later royal residences are not of the quality of their lost predecessors, and England is almost the only country in Europe devoid of a great eighteenth-century royal palace. It is therefore an architectural tragedy that so many of the ancient palaces of the Kings of England were destroyed in the seventeenth century, during the Civil War and its aftermath. Hardly a stone remains of Woodstock, Clarendon, King's Langley, Sheen/Richmond, Greenwich, Oatlands and Nonsuch, and only fragments of Winchester, Edward III's Windsor, Westminster, Whitehall and Eltham.

The royal residences of Britain have an interest beyond their basic architectural quality. They represent the longest continuous tradition in Europe, apart from the papacy, and form the framework to the oldest and grandest surviving monarchy. Their story reflects the development and vicissitudes of that monarchy over a period of a thousand years; from the semi-divine chiefs of the invading tribes of the Dark Ages, the perambulating government machine of the most advanced monarchy in medieval Europe, the Tudor and Stuart attempt at absolutism, and the political revolutions of the seventeenth century, to the emergence of modern constitutional monarchy and the transformation of the monarch into a kind of glorified country gentleman. The royal residences have developed with the institution of monarchy, and reflect its history in their architecture.

THE EARLY MIDDLE AGES

The history of the English royal residences begins with the emergence of the Anglo-Saxon monarchies from the shadows of pagan tribalism, and the establishment of the Christian kingdoms of Northumbria, Mercia and Wessex, and then the political kingdom of England. By the time that Bede was completing his History in 731, all England south of the Humber was united under King Aethelbald of Mercia, who in 746 assumed the title of Rex Britannia. Mercia, however, broke up in the face of the Viking invasions, and the following century saw the rise of Wessex as a bulwark of native resistance to the Vikings. It was under the aegis of the kings of Wessex, of the house of Cerdic, that the geographical and political kingdom of England took shape in the ninth century and developed into the most advanced monarchy in Europe. Wessex was distinguished by a long line of kings of remarkable quality: Alfred the Great, Edward the Elder, Athelstan, Edmund, Eadred, Eadwig and Edgar. Under them England south of the Humber formed one kingdom with effective laws, coinage of a quality not equalled elsewhere, and an embryo system of taxation. Their court was distinguished for its high standard of literacy. Alfred in particular was a patron of learning and religion. He sponsored a programme of translations of philosophical, religious and historical works into English as well as codifying the King's Laws. The ultimate submission of this sophisticated monarchy to the Vikings did not alter its character, for King Canute took over what he found and merely strengthened it further. He established the king's guards, the Housecarles, who formed the spearhead of the army, and reinforced and further codified the King's Law.

Nothing survives of the residences of the pre-Norman English kings, though they were notable patrons of architecture and their houses must have reflected the general sophistication of their courts. What little is known about them is the result of archaeological excavations and literary references. The Saxon kings had no fixed capital but moved from estate to estate with their court, staying in one place for only as long as the food lasted, though in the tenth century the King's treasure remained at Winchester, giving it a degree of pre-eminence, while Edward the Confessor's favourite house was Westminster near London where he rebuilt the Benedictine abbey. In general the King's Houses, the 'domi regis' or 'villae Regales', were situated all over the country. They comprised loosely grouped buildings round a hall, often more like a little village within a fortified enclosure than one unified building. The hall was the principal room.

There the king dined, met his advisers, and received emissaries from the pope and the emperor. It remained the hub of the English court for hundreds of years.

Two pre-Norman palaces have been excavated – the seventh-century palace at Yeavering in Northumbria and the ninth-century palace at Cheddar in Wessex. The centrepiece of Yeavering was a great aisled hall two storeys high with plastered walls and four central doors. The latter recall the well-known paragraph in Bede where human life is compared to the passage of a bird through a lighted hall, flying in at one door from the darkness into the light, then out through the opposite door into the darkness again. The most interesting feature at Yeavering was the Moot Place, a banked semi-circular layout of wooden seats like a Roman amphitheatre, and obviously derived from one. The buildings at Yeavering were set within a fortified enclosure, but those at Cheddar were not. Cheddar too consisted of a complex of timber buildings grouped round a two-storeyed hall, 76 feet long by 18 feet wide, and a bower or private chamber of the King, 28 feet by 22 feet. The details of the interior fitting up of these buildings are not known, but it is probable that the walls of the King's Halls and bowers were hung with tapestry. In *Beowulf*, for instance, there is reference to a hall hung with 'gold-inwoven tapestries'.[1]

The Norman Conquest strengthened the English monarchy in various ways. William I enormously enlarged its economic base by creating a royal estate which comprised a third of all the land in the country. He also superimposed continental feudalism on top of the Anglo-Saxon system, but without eradicating the older inheritance. The Anglo-Norman kings were the powerful suzerains of a strong military baronage as well as national or tribal kings in the older sense, with the wider popular support which that implied. Perhaps most importantly, they were also lords of a wider political hegemony than England itself. For the whole of the medieval period, the English Crown held sway over an empire made up in addition to England, of Ireland and Wales and fluctuating continental possessions, varying at different times from nearly the whole of France, at its widest extent under Henry V, to Calais only by the end of the fifteenth century. This wider responsibility of the king meant that for long periods he was absent abroad, especially during the twelfth century. This combination of an advanced, powerful and international monarchy obviously had important repercussions on the character of the English royal residences.

The Anglo-Norman kings took over the existing Saxon royal houses including the major establishments with King's Halls at Westminster, Gloucester and Winchester as well as the lesser houses such as Cheddar, Brigstock and Woodstock, but they added many more hunting lodges, especially in the new royal forests like Clarendon in Wiltshire, and a large number of castles, the latter a Norman introduction into England. Some of these castles were purely military, but some were palace-towers or hall-keeps intended for the accommodation of the King as well as being military strongholds. The chief residential castle founded by the Conqueror was the Tower of London. It was begun as a hasty defence thrown up in 1067 to hold London for the new King, but ten years later the original timber and earth fortifications were replaced with the magnificent palace-tower of Caen stone (from Normandy) which still dominates the whole complex today. The erection of this rectangular keep, three storeys high with walls fifteen feet thick, was supervised by a celebrated castle builder, Bishop Gandulf of Rochester. It contained all the essential accommodation of a royal residence including a Great Hall and an apsidal chapel with arcades of

The Tower of London.
Exterior of the White
Tower built by Bishop
Gandulf for William I in
1077.

Below: The Tower of
London. St John's Chapel
in the White Tower.

strong cylindrical piers. The compact grandeur of the Tower was a new departure in the English royal residences. Nothing like it had been seen since the grandiose days of the Roman occupation of Britain. The first formal record of a king keeping his court in the Tower is Stephen, who stayed there during the civil war over his accession. From this developed the tradition of a new king spending a few days at the Tower before processing through the City on his coronation day to Westminster Abbey, a tradition which lasted down to the sixteenth century, though by then the Tower had become more of a state prison than a palace.

The Norman and Angevin kings were constantly on the move, riding from manor to manor and castle to castle in order to satisfy the needs of administration, as well as for hunting and recreation. This restless existence made the King's presence felt all over the country and was an important aspect of royal policy. The King's movements displayed a certain regularity and were obviously organized with care and forethought. It was customary for the court to celebrate Christmas and the other great feasts in particular places. William I when in England wore his crown three times a year – at Easter at Winchester, at Whitsuntide at Westminster, and at Christmas at Gloucester. On these occasions he entertained all the great men of England, archbishops, bishops, abbots, earls, thanes and knights, and made important proclamations. The Domesday Survey, for instance, was ordered at Gloucester in 1085. William II, 'Rufus', carried on this custom; so did Henry I in a modified form.[2] There must have been halls at Westminster, Winchester and Gloucester, therefore, capable of accommodating these great feudal gatherings. The site of the royal hall at Gloucester is uncertain. At Winchester, William the Conqueror is known to have rebuilt the hall, together with the rest of the Saxon palace, in the fourth year of his reign and to have erected defensive earthworks and a motte. But only traces of the latter remain, while the hall itself was replaced in the thirteenth century. Of these three great halls, only that at Westminster, constructed by William II in the 1090s (completed by 1099), still stands.

Westminster Hall is 240 feet long and 67 feet wide. It was (and is) the largest hall in England and probably the largest in Europe. This vast size gave it a pre-eminence which it was never to lose and marked it as the ceremonial centre of the Anglo-Norman kingdom. At first Westminster shared with Winchester the distinction of being the principal royal residence in England, just as Rouen was in Normandy, but gradually it took over from Winchester and became the sole centre of royal government, and the administrative capital of England. Though re-roofed by Richard II, Westminster Hall has never been enlarged and the walls are substantially Norman. Originally it was lit by a tier of Romanesque windows set in an arcaded wall gallery which ran round three sides of the interior, and the timber roof was supported on wooden posts which divided the space into three aisles. Externally the walls were articulated by shallow buttresses forming twelve bays, and there were decorative bands of chequered stonework beneath the windows. It is possible that the new hall may have been built round the older timber one which continued in use till the new walls were completed.[3]

These three halls catered for the ceremonial occasions when the Norman kings appeared in state surrounded by their barons. At other times, when they were in England, they lived in castles or hunting lodges near the tracts of country where forest law preserved the game for royal sport – the castles at Windsor, Salisbury (Old Sarum), Corfe (Dorset), Norwich (Norfolk) and Chelmsford (Essex), and the unfortified manors at Woodstock (Oxfordshire), Odiham

Westminster Hall. Detail of an original window from William Rufus's hall.

(Hampshire), Alverton (Gloucestershire), King's Cliffe (Northamptonshire), Brampton (Huntingdonshire), and Dunstable (Bedfordshire). The government moved round with the King just as it had under the Saxons. Minimal records, sealing wax, parchment and itinerant clerks followed him from place to place. Only the treasure, for obvious reasons, did not move but remained at Winchester in conditions of permanent security.

The large-scale absenteeism on the continent of the Angevin kings in the twelfth century led to a rapid development of certain aspects of the government. This made localization inevitable, and the new permanent government departments found a home at Westminster, not at Winchester. The most elaborate organ of the Angevin government was the King's office of audit and account known as the Exchequer. It was founded by Henry I and was given control of the royal seal. It kept permanent records, the Exchequer Rolls, which formed the first regular accounting system in Europe. By the reign of Henry II, Westminster had become the normal place for the biennial sessions of the Exchequer and a subsidiary treasury was also established there. By the time of King John, this had absorbed the Winchester treasury. Under Henry II there were also great developments of the law with the creation of a real royal criminal and civil law; permanent legal records began to be kept from approximately 1181. This gradual formalization of the King's Law led to its more important functions being fixed at Westminster. At different dates both the Court of Common Pleas and the Court of the King's Bench came to be housed in Westminster Hall. Already by the twelfth century Westminster had acquired its unique status among English royal palaces not just as the residence of the King but as the home of the first regular government departments in western Europe.[4] As a result Westminster developed into a palace unlike any other. The accommodation was progressively enlarged and adapted to meet the administrative requirements of the Crown till the original hall had become the nucleus of a large complex of accretions containing almost every department of English government, as well as the principal royal residence. It was only in the sixteenth century, following fire damage to the private apartments, that Henry VIII transferred his court to Whitehall, leaving Westminster to the government officials alone.

Henry II was a great builder at all his residences. Abbot Robert de Torigni of Mont St Michel wrote in 1161 that 'not only in Normandy but also in England, in the Duchy of Aquitaine, in the County of Anjou, in Maine and Touraine, he either repaired old castles and palaces or built new ones'. The royal records from the reign of Henry II onwards provide 'something more than a rough guide', though not the total cost, of the King's building work, and so give a clear idea of the development of the royal residences. At Westminster he built an additional Great Hall called the New Hall, or sometimes the Lesser or the White Hall. It was smaller than Westminster Hall and situated to its west, and was intended for domestic use, leaving the old hall for great state ceremonies such as coronation banquets and official business like the law sessions. Henry also built chambers for himself and his wife, a King's Wardrobe, cloister, kitchen, the Exchequer Office (a two-storeyed building in stone), and a quay along the river front in 1179–80.[5]

At Windsor he replaced the timber buildings of William the Conqueror with stone walls and erected the Round Tower on top of the motte. Perhaps the most interesting developments in his reign took place at the unfortified residences, or King's Manors, which came to be increasingly preferred to his castles by Henry

II, as is attested by the sums of money lavished on them and also by the great political events which made the names of Clarendon and Woodstock part of English history.[6]

Under Henry II Woodstock and Clarendon joined Westminster as the most important English royal palaces together with the two palace-castles of Windsor and Winchester. They were rambling, incoherent complexes of buildings and courtyards – halls, chapels, chambers, and kitchens. They both had aisled Great Halls divided by stone piers with carved Romanesque capitals, their windows and doorways elaborately carved. Bits of chevron carving from Woodstock have been found in the rubble filling the piers of Vanbrugh's bridge at Blenheim. The dimensions of the Clarendon Hall are known: it was 83 feet long and 51 feet wide. Both houses had approximately similar layouts, with the kitchen at one end of the hall and the royal apartments at the other. The chapel was the most important of the buildings. It was in the King's Chapel according to the Constitutions of Clarendon that elections to vacant bishoprics and abbacies in the King's gift were to take place. Just as the chapel in the royal residences was used for the exercise of the King's ecclesiastical rights, so his private apartments were used for secular business, and the names of the rooms came to be perpetuated in the early government departments – curia, camera, guarderoba. The chief of the private apartments was the King's Chamber, which served as his bedroom as well as his private day room. It was elaborately decorated, usually with wall paintings. At Winchester, for example, Henry commanded a mural depicting the tragedy of his life in the new chamber built 1176–9. A brood of four eaglets (his sons) was depicted preying on the parent bird, and one, the fourth, was poised on the neck, watching intently for the moment to peck out his eyes.

In a class by itself was a subsidiary house called Everswell built by Henry II in Woodstock Park. It is traditionally reputed to have been built for the King's mistress Rosamund Clifford, and was planned round a spring from which the water ran through a series of three rectangular pools surrounded by cloistered walks. Nothing else like this is known to have existed in northern Europe, but there are grounds for thinking that it was inspired by the palaces near Palermo in the Norman kingdom of Sicily, with which Henry II's court had many contacts. Today only the Moorish Alhambra at Granada can give any idea of what Everswell may have been like. There was nothing to compare with it in France. The overall design of an enclosed garden with chambers and pools may have been inspired by *Tristan and Isolde* (which was probably written for Henry II) though it is possible that the influence was the other way round. In any case, the two are clearly related to each other and both are the product of a cosmopolitan and intellectually sophisticated court.[7] Among the exotic features of Woodstock was a menagerie which contained a porcupine and other strange animals.

In addition to the major royal houses in the twelfth century, there were a large number of lesser manors or 'hunting lodges', each with its official custodian who was paid an annual salary of 30s 5d. Richard I's new lodge at Kinver in Staffordshire is a good example, and gives an idea of the character and accommodation of this type of smaller royal house. It contained a hall with adjacent offices and kitchen and a King's Chamber. There was also a gaol for the imprisonment of poachers and other forest offenders, and a fish pond to supply carp and bream to the royal table on Fridays and fast days. These buildings stood within an enclosure surrounded by a palisade sixteen feet high.

This and all the other buildings at Kinver were constructed of timber. The total cost was £28 18s 9d. Nearly all the smaller manor houses were rebuilt or enlarged by the Angevins in the twelfth and early thirteenth centuries, partly in response to the enlargement of the area covered by the royal forests. In the course of his reign John accumulated the largest number of houses possessed by any medieval English king. He inherited twenty-three from Richard I and took five or six more from their owners (without compensation). He was forced to give up some of these as part of the Magna Carta settlement in 1215 and 1216, but he left over twenty houses to his successor, King Henry III.

Henry III, who came of age in 1227 and married Eleanor of Provence in 1236, was the greatest builder among the English medieval kings. He took a strong personal interest in all his residences and in the collections of jewels, relics and works of art which they contained. He spent £3,000 per annum, a tenth of his annual income, on building. It was more than he could afford. It was of course inevitable that any medieval king should be a patron of artists and builders. But what distinguishes Henry III from nearly all other English monarchs was the close personal aesthetic interest he took in his works. He was a King with a highly developed aesthetic sense, which he gratified on a truly royal scale. For though he was not able to get his own way politically, he could and did get his own way in his magnificent architectural projects. There have been rulers such as Louis XIV, Catherine the Great, most popes, or nearer home Edward III and Henry VIII, for whom architecture and the decorative arts have been an expression – in some cases almost an instrument – of political power. But for others such as George IV, the Bourbon kings of Spain or Ludwig II of Bavaria, the arts have been a substitute for the power which eluded them. Henry III belonged rather more to this latter category than to the former. He took refuge from his inadequacy as a ruler in those schemes of building and decoration which have made his reign 'as celebrated in the history of art as it is inglorious politically'. He was a better judge of sculpture and painting than of men. Building was always in the forefront of his mind. Wherever he was, his clerks were called to take down writs which read more like architect's specifications than government documents, writs abounding in adjectives like *decens*, *pulcher*, and *sumptuosus*. Even during the disastrous Gascon expedition of 1242–3, he found time to send detailed directions for the completion of his new chapel at Windsor Castle. In England he was constantly on the move from house to house inspecting building work. It is one of the tragedies of English art history that so little of what he built survives. Plans of Westminster and Havering can be reconstructed from documentary evidence, while the layouts at Clarendon, Clipstone and Writtle have been excavated. But only the smallest fragments of his palaces actually exist – some mutilated arches and a window at Windsor, the over-restored hall at Winchester, the tiled floor from the chapel at Clarendon. It is Westminster Abbey which has come down to us as Henry III's supreme memorial, not any of his palaces.

The houses upon which his expenditure was greatest were Windsor (£15,000), Westminster (£10,000), Clarendon (£3,600), Woodstock (£3,300), Havering (£2,000), Guildford (£1,800). Large sums were also spent on the 'hunting lodges' at Brill, Clipstone, Feckenham, Freemantle, Geddington and Silverston. In the course of his reign he spent at least £38,000 on his houses, which was more than double the expenditure under John. Most of Henry's buildings were of stone, though some of the smaller ones were of timber. All the houses which he inherited had Great Halls and kitchen offices. His own additions comprised new private chambers, chapels, wardrobes and privies for himself and his Queen, and also for his eldest son, the Lord Edward. He also greatly improved the standards of comfort in all his houses, adding porches to the halls to keep out draughts and glazing all the windows, adding iron bars as well to repel intruders after an incident at Woodstock in September 1238 when a madman climbed into the King's Chamber armed with a knife intending to murder him, 'but by God's providence He was with the Queen' at the time. As well as being an aesthete, Henry was extremely pious. He went to Mass three times a day, which even St Louis thought a trifle excessive. This religious fervour was expressed in the chapels he built. In nearly all his houses he provided separate chapels for himself and the Queen, and sometimes a small oratory connected with his chamber as well. Altogether he maintained fifty chapels for the exclusive use of himself and his wife. He embellished the older ones with stained glass, wall paintings, statuary and metalwork, and built eighteen completely new chapels.[8]

Henry III's favourite palace was Westminster, and he spent more time there out of his peripatetic existence than any of his predecessors. He lavished large sums of money on additions and embellishments, making it the finest royal palace in Europe. His best-known work at Westminster was a new King's Great Chamber, known from its decoration as the Painted Chamber. It must have

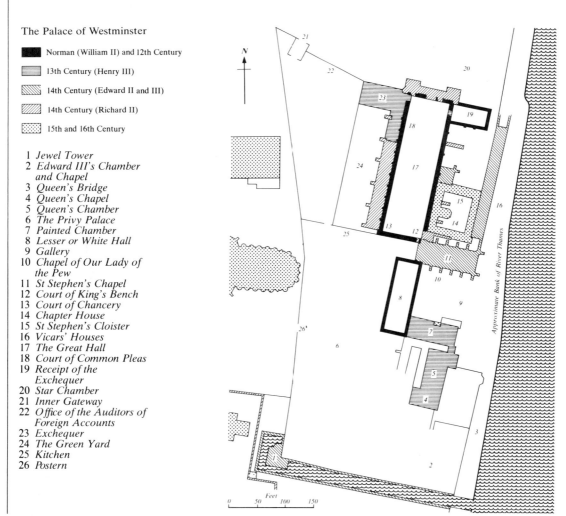

The Palace of Westminster

Norman (William II) and 12th Century

13th Century (Henry III)

14th Century (Edward II and III)

14th Century (Richard II)

15th and 16th Century

1 *Jewel Tower*
2 *Edward III's Chamber and Chapel*
3 *Queen's Bridge*
4 *Queen's Chapel*
5 *Queen's Chamber*
6 *The Privy Palace*
7 *Painted Chamber*
8 *Lesser or White Hall*
9 *Gallery*
10 *Chapel of Our Lady of the Pew*
11 *St Stephen's Chapel*
12 *Court of King's Bench*
13 *Court of Chancery*
14 *Chapter House*
15 *St Stephen's Cloister*
16 *Vicars' Houses*
17 *The Great Hall*
18 *Court of Common Pleas*
19 *Receipt of the Exchequer*
20 *Star Chamber*
21 *Inner Gateway*
22 *Office of the Auditors of Foreign Accounts*
23 *Exchequer*
24 *The Green Yard*
25 *Kitchen*
26 *Postern*

1. 'The Coronation of Edward the Confessor' in the Painted Chamber, Westminster Palace. Water Colour by Edward Crocker.

2. St Stephens, Westminster Palace. The Lower Chapel.

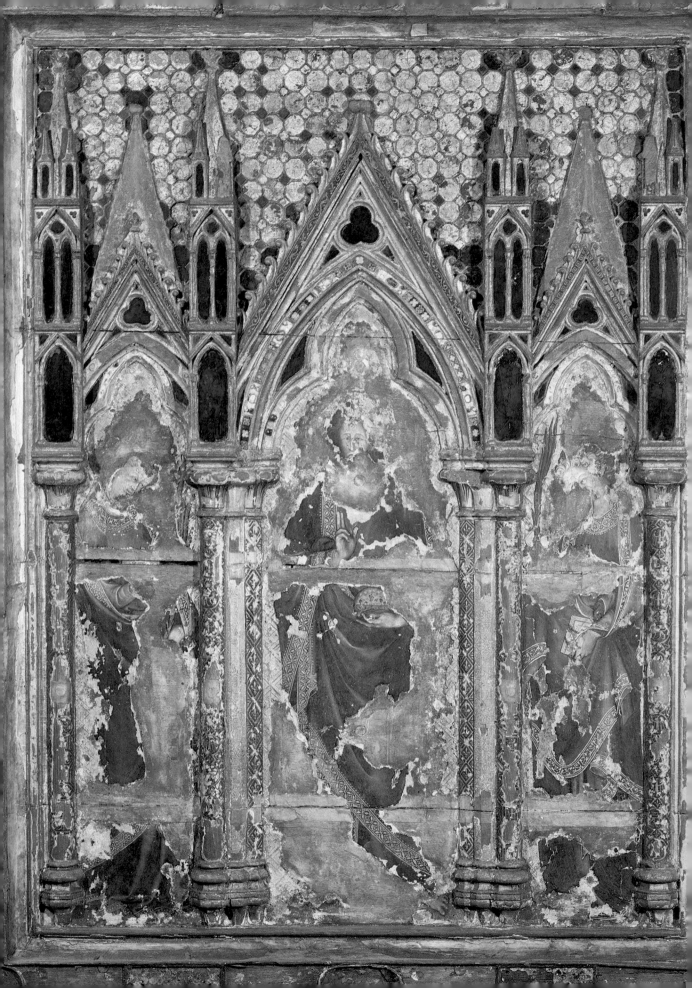

3. OPPOSITE: *The Westminster Retable.*

4. RIGHT: *The Inner Gateway, Windsor Castle. Watercolour by Paul Sandby.*

5. BELOW: *Eltham Palace. Exterior.*

6. OVERLEAF: *Interior of the Great Hall, Eltham Palace.*

been a most impressive interior: 80 feet long by 26 feet wide and 31 feet high. It had a timber ceiling of 'one regular and beautiful pattern', a wall fireplace, and a tiled floor, as well as splendid wall paintings begun in 1236. The principal article of furniture was the King's bed, a canopied structure supported on green-painted posts sprinkled with gold stars and with green curtains. The floor tiles of reddish brown with inlaid yellow patterns were a novelty. Henry III introduced their manufacture into England from Anjou and Poitou specially to embellish his palaces. Such tiles were of high quality, as can be judged from the surviving floor of the Chapter House at Westminster Abbey, perhaps the finest example of medieval floor tiling in existence. The murals, executed by Master William of Westminster (a Benedictine monk) and Master Walter of Durham (a layman) together with the latter's son Thomas, covered the entire surface of the walls. The dado was treated as a *trompe-l'œil* green curtain. The walls above were painted in six bands of Old Testament stories and the life of Edward the Confessor, culminating in a magnificent scene of his coronation, much enriched with gold-leaf and inset with blue glass and other coloured inlays. Their workmanship was of 'the highest technical excellence' and created a very splendid effect.[9] They were the finest expression of the court style of Henry III and are one of the high water marks of English medieval art. The King took a

Palace of Westminster. The Painted Chamber built by Henry III in 1236.

Above: Palace of Westminster. Undercroft of the Painted Chamber.

Above right: Palace of Westminster. Detail of *trompe l'oeil* painted drapery in the Queen's Chamber.

Palace of Westminster. The Lesser Hall. This later was adapted to form the House of Lords and the ceiling shown here was designed by Inigo Jones in the early 17th century.

keen interest in the mural decorations of his palaces and himself specified the subjects. Many of them formed part of the common stock of medieval iconography, though the preoccupation with the memory of Edward the Confessor, who had founded Westminster Palace and had died there, was special to Henry III. In the little oratory off the Painted Chamber the walls were painted with scenes from the life of St Joseph, and there was a little round window in the dividing wall so that the King could see the altar from his bed.

Henry also provided new apartments for Queen Eleanor at Westminster in 1237–8. They formed a two-storeyed block with a low vaulted ground floor, to the south of the Painted Chamber. The main rooms on the first floor were a chapel, a chamber and a wardrobe, all with cheerful painted decoration. The chapel was 43 feet long by 21 feet wide and was approached through a porch with two richly moulded doorways. It was lit by eight lancet windows, the east window formed of triple lancets with carved and coloured portrait heads of the young King and Queen as corbels. The font and the altar were both of Purbeck marble. Henry III made few structural alterations to the two King's Chapels or the two Great Halls at Westminster, but he enriched them with new decorations.

At the Tower of London, Henry III completed the stone curtain wall and built a new palace south-east of the Conqueror's White Tower, complete with a Great Hall, King's Chamber, Privy Closet, galleries and gardens. Various embellishments were also made to the older buildings. The Chapel of St John had stained glass installed in its windows. The Queen's Chamber was painted with a pattern of roses. Henry also began the menagerie which remained in the Tower till the early nineteenth century, when it was removed to Regent's Park and became the London Zoo. It was composed chiefly of exotic gifts from other European monarchs. Three leopards were sent by the Emperor Frederick II in 1235. They were joined shortly afterwards by a camel, and then by a polar bear from Norway. King Louis IX of France presented an elephant, but he pined, and died after only three years in London.

Under Henry III the chief country palaces were Clarendon, Woodstock and Guildford, together with Windsor and Winchester Castles. Henry III continued the enlargement and enrichment of Clarendon begun under Henry II. He added new Queen's apartments, a King's Chamber, a new kitchen, and private chapels for the King and the Queen (in addition to Henry II's Great Chapel), as well as quarters for the King's eldest son, knights in attendance and chaplains. He also doubled the size of the Great Wine Cellar. The result was a rambling and picturesque complex of buildings without any concept of formal planning or overall monumental effect. The relative positions of the various buildings were either determined by long-established custom, or were spontaneous. The new rooms at Clarendon were as richly decorated as at Westminster with tiled floors and painted walls and ceilings. Part of the magnificent circular tiled floor from the King's Chapel is now at the British Museum, together with one of the original kilns for firing the tiles discovered when the site was excavated in 1937. The King's Chapel and his Great Chamber or Antioch Chamber were the two most elaborately decorated rooms in the King's apartments. The latter had a ceiling painted green and spangled with gilded lead stars (some of which came to light in 1937), and the walls were painted with romantic crusading stories showing the siege of Antioch. Henry III took the cross in 1250 but never went to the Holy Land himself. The Alexander Chamber also took its name from its wallpaintings, which depicted the story of Alexander the Great.[10]

Top: Clarendon Palace. Tiled floor from the King's Chapel.

Above: Clarendon Palace. Tiled floor from the Queen's Chamber.

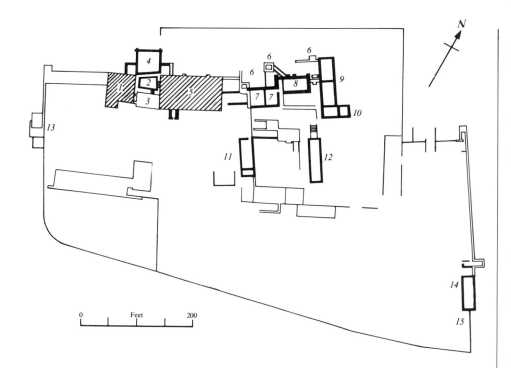

Clarendon Palace,
Wiltshire, as excavated
in 1937

 Henry III

Twelfth Century

1 *King's Kitchen*
2 *Cloister*
3 *Larder*
4 *Household Kitchen*
5 *Great Hall*
6 *Privy*
7 *King's Chambers*
8 *Antioch Chamber*
9 *Queen's Chambers*
10 *Chapel*
11 *Alexander Chamber*
12 *Great Wine Cellar*
13 *West Gateway*
14 *Barn*
15 *Site of East Gateway*

Henry was equally active at Guildford in Surrey, where he made a new royal residence near the old castle, and one which rapidly became one of his favourites. The nucleus was a hall with aisles of timber columns painted to look like black Purbeck marble. He added a new kitchen in 1244 and King's and Queen's Chambers. The Queen's was painted green with gold stars. The King's was whitewashed and diapered, the ceiling painted green and sprinkled with gold and silver stars. A chamber, 50 feet by 26 feet, with large windows and green-painted wainscot, was built for the Lord Edward in 1246. A new porch was erected in 1248, and in 1256 the hall was rebuilt following a fire, this time with real Purbeck marble columns and paintings showing the parable of Dives and Lazarus, a religious subject which much appealed to the King. Also in 1246 a cloister with Purbeck marble columns was built in the garden. There were also two chapels within the precincts, but the exact layout of all these buildings is not known.

At Woodstock, too, Henry made huge improvements. He increased the number of chapels from one to six – a Great Chapel, a Round Chapel, the Chapel of St John of Woodstock, the Chapel of St Edward, the King's Chapel, and the Queen's Chapel. He also built new chambers for the Lord Edward and the Queen, and wardrobes for himself and the Queen, as well as new kitchen offices. The Queen's Chamber at Woodstock was the earliest recorded building in England to have ornamental battlements, thus starting a fashion which was to become such a characteristic feature of English domestic architecture in the later Middle Ages. Another fashion started by Henry III was the decorative use of heraldry. The gardens at Woodstock and Everswell were further embellished, a hundred pear trees, for example, being planted in the Queen's Garden in 1264.[11]

At Windsor Henry completed the circuit of stone walls, built new royal apartments and a King's Chapel. These buildings were in the lower not the upper ward, and fragments of them survive embedded in the collegiate buildings

Woodstock Palace as it was shortly before its demolition.

Windsor Castle. Water colour by John Buckler showing Henry II's Round Tower and Gerard's Tower built by Henry III.

and cloisters behind the present St George's Chapel. Windsor was the only one of Henry's palaces to have a compact and coherent plan, a feature dictated by shortage of space within the castle walls. His new apartments and chapel were arranged round a courtyard with cloister walks. The King's Chapel at Windsor was the largest and most imposing of the private chapels that Henry III built for himself. It was 70 feet long and 28 feet wide, and must have been comparable with Louis IX's Sainte Chapelle in Paris. It was destroyed in the reign of Henry VII without being recorded, but is known to have had a timber vault painted to look like stone and the west doors with magnificent ironwork by Gilebertus survive. Henry III visited Paris for the first time in 1254, and it was the Sainte Chapelle that he most wanted to see. A contemporary poem makes him declare that if he could, he would like to put it in a cart and bring it home with him. But by the time of the Paris visit, the Windsor chapel was already complete, so there can have been no direct influence. Henry also built a Queen's Chapel at Windsor, but even less is known about that, save that it was two-storeyed, with the Queen's pew in an upper gallery and space for her household below. All the new rooms at Windsor were decorated with the usual biblical and historical subjects. The Queen's Chamber had its walls painted with the Tree of Jesse, while the ceiling was green with gold stars.

Windsor Castle. An archway from Henry III's chapel.

The west door of Henry
III's chapel at Windsor.

Right: Windsor. Detail of
the decorative ironwork by
Gilebertus on the west
door of Henry III's chapel.

Below: Winchester Palace.
Exterior of the Great Hall
completed in 1235.

Winchester, though now subordinate to Westminster in the hierarchy of the
royal residences and no longer the home of the treasury, remained a favourite
royal residence. Henry carried out a radical transformation there too. The
earliest work at Winchester was a new Great Hall, the roof supported on
Purbeck marble columns and the walls punctuated with tall transomed two-
light windows. It was completed in 1235 and is the only palace building from the

Top: Winchester Palace. Interior of the Great Hall, the roof supported on columns of Purbeck marble.

Above: Winchester Palace. Detail of a hall window.

reign of Henry III to survive intact, though drastically 'restored' in the nineteenth century. The interior was originally painted white and lined in red to resemble masonry, and there was a Mappa Mundi and a Wheel of Fortune, two favourite medieval subjects. Henry also beautified the five private chapels and provided new quarters for himself and the Queen with his favourite green and gold wainscotting and Purbeck marble chimneypieces, but nothing survives of any of that.

In all his works Henry III relied heavily on his two artistic advisers, Elias of Derham, an eminent ecclesiastic and 'incomparabilis artifix', and Edward of Westminster, a royal servant. The latter was the King's right-hand man in all that appealed to the pious and artistic side of his character. In 1240 he took his father's place as Keeper of Works at Westminster, and for the next twenty-five years was the channel through which all the King's schemes for improving Westminster were set in motion, as can be seen from the numerous surviving instructions in the Close Rolls in the Public Record Office. For example: 'The King to Edward of Westminster, greeting. Since we recall that you told us that it would be rather more splendid to make the two leopards which are to be on either side of our throne at Westminster of bronze instead of cutting them out of marble, we command you to have them made of metal as you said and to have the steps before the throne made of cut stone.'[12] The death of Edward of Westminster in 1265 brought to an end the King's great programme of architectural improvements and marked the end of an era in the history of the English royal residences.

II

THE LATER MIDDLE AGES

The development of the English royal residences between the death of Henry III in 1272 and the accession to the throne of Henry VII in 1485 forms a complex story reflecting the vicissitudes of the Crown in that period with alternating strong and weak monarchs, though in some cases the latter were nearly as active patrons of architecture as the former. It is a story of fluctuating acquisition and alienation. Many old houses were disposed of, while other new ones were acquired by the Crown. Of the twenty country houses inherited by Edward I in 1272, only six were still in the possession of the Crown in 1485 – Clarendon, Clipstone, Havering, Windsor and Woodstock. These figures do not include such old residential castles as Winchester, which though retained by the Crown were not much used in the later Middle Ages. The palaces most favoured by the Kings of England in the fourteenth century, apart from Westminster and Windsor, included Eltham, King's Langley and Sheen, all of which were new royal possessions. Between 1272 and 1485, some twenty-five other houses were held and maintained by the Crown for longer or shorter periods but were of lesser importance in the general royal galaxy. Some of them were acquired by bequest, escheat, gift or purchase, while others came to the Crown from their original owners by forfeiture. Some were retained for good, while others were granted out again to royal favourites and supporters. Thus the total number of royal residences in the later Middle Ages was far from constant. Under Edward II and in the early years of Edward III it rose to twenty-four or twenty-five, but thereafter declined. Between 1355 and 1377 there was a substantial reduction by alienation and demolition. In the later fourteenth century Richard II maintained sixteen or seventeen houses. The Lancastrians kept up only about a dozen, and the Yorkists only nine or ten. So by the fifteenth century the number of royal residences was appreciably smaller than it had been in the thirteenth century.[1]

The reduction in the numbers of the royal houses in the second half of this period reflected a relative decline in the economic position of the Crown, and also a decline in the personal calibre of the English kings. From 1377 onwards the character of individual monarchs was less than an asset to the Crown. There was only one good king – Henry V – and two reasonable mediocrities – the Lancastrian Henry IV and the Yorkist Edward IV. The others were more or less incompetent and there were no less than five violent changes of monarchs. The medieval government machine was at the height of its development, but individual kings were not able to handle it properly. The disastrous reign of the pious but incompetent Henry VI marked the nadir of the prestige of the medieval monarchy. The late fourteenth and fifteenth-century Kings of England were, on the whole, poorer than those of the twelfth and thirteenth centuries; they also derived less of their income from the direct exploitation of territorial estates than their predecessors, and more from taxation. The Black Death in the mid-fourteenth century led to a general economic crisis which affected the finances of the Crown more than those of the great nobles. The latter were dwindling in numbers and as a result growing richer through the amalgamation of estates as the survivors married the heiresses of extinct peers. The gap between the Crown and the great landowners was therefore decreasing, to the detriment of the former's relative dignity. The Hundred Years War with France greatly overstretched the Crown's military and financial resources, while the ignominious defeat of the English in 1453 left the Crown with debts of £372,000, about five times its annual income. This resulted in near-bankruptcy and made drastic economies essential, Henry VI's court in particular being notorious for its threadbare quality. The story of fifteenth-century decline was partly reversed by Edward IV's carefully planned economies and reform of the royal household.

Another significant development in the royal residences in the later Middle Ages, in addition to their contraction, was a marked shift in their distribution. In the reign of Edward I they had been scattered all over the Midlands and south of England, as they had been since Saxon times, and they had still catered for the needs of a court that was always on the move from one part of the country to another, such royal perambulations forming part of the regular government administration. But the houses that the later medieval kings chose to retain or acquire were all within one day's ride of London. By the accession of Richard II in 1377, Clipstone was the only royal residence remaining north of the Chilterns, and by the fifteenth century the houses of the Kings of England were largely confined to the Thames Valley, setting the pattern which survived down to Queen Victoria. Though the Lancastrians had houses of their own on their northern estates they hardly ever used them, and when they travelled north they either stayed in castles or at monasteries. This concentration of the royal residences in the later Middle Ages was a result of the increasing centralization of the royal government at Westminster, which became in this period the administrative capital, as well as the chief residence, of the Kings of England.

Edward I who succeeded Henry III in 1272 was a strong and capable king. He conducted successful wars of consolidation in Wales and Gascony, though he was less successful in Scotland; and perhaps most notably was responsible for much important law-making, earning the nickname of the 'English Justinian'. He was also a great builder. His most ambitious architectural project was the programme of eight new castles in Wales and the reconstruction, at a cost of £10,000, of the fortifications of the Tower of London, but he also continued his father's work at the various royal residences. He spent £2,000 on further improvements at Windsor Castle and no less than £10,000 on Westminster Palace. His work at the latter included the elaboration of the piped water supply which his father had installed. In 1287 a new 'lavatory' was made inside the lesser hall, with marble columns 'subtly wrought', statues of 'gilt tin' and a tin cup for drinking water. The bathrooms in the royal apartments were also re-done and new bath tubs with gilded taps supplied for the King and the Queen.

The major new work at Westminster, however, was not plumbing but the construction of a new royal chapel dedicated to St Stephen. It took fifty-six years to complete and was to become the most splendid chapel in England. The existing Norman chapel was considered unworthy of the palace especially when compared with the French King's new Sainte-Chapelle in Paris, which provided the inspiration for Edward I's St Stephen's Chapel. It had a similar two-storeyed layout, with the main chapel on the first floor and a subsidiary chapel below. This two-tier arrangement was the standard plan for medieval palace chapels. The upper chapel was intended for the exclusive use of the royal family, while the lower one was for the court at large. The lower chapel was begun in 1292, but only the walls had been built when work stopped in 1297 on the outbreak of war with Scotland and the diversion of all the available funds to Edward's military campaign in the north. The tops of the walls were protected from the frost with temporary thatching and the continuation of the work, including the vault of the lower chapel and all the upper chapel, was left to his successors. Edward's foundations and walls however determined the overall proportions and form of the chapel as completed. It was a rectangle 90 feet long and 30 feet wide, running south towards the river from the west end of Westminster Hall. At the liturgically 'west' end (actually north) was a large double porch. The building materials, both stone and timber, for St Stephen's Chapel were brought by water from the royal estates in France.[2]

Edward I died in the middle of his Scottish campaign and was succeeded by his eldest son, Edward II. The new King had a very different character to his father and lacked his military and political acumen. He was an ineffective administrator and did not get on with his barons, who disapproved of his low tastes, such as swimming. This led in the end to his deposition and murder. Though a weak King, he was an aesthete and spent heavily on his houses, continuing the momentum of his father and grandfather's building work. His magnificent coronation formed the overture to much that followed. It was stage-managed by the King's favourite Piers Gaveston, whose fancy habits included eating with a fork, and who, to the disapproval of the barons, had a prominent place in the coronation procession dressed in cloth of gold. Fourteen temporary halls were erected, and forty ovens constructed at Westminster for the coronation banquet. Edward II's more solid work at Westminster was nearly as ambitious. He spent a further £7,000 on the palace, and continued work at St Stephen's Chapel from 1320 to 1326. He vaulted the lower chapel with what is generally regarded as the earliest lierne vault in England, though its carved bosses are rather crude for such a regal commission. Edward II also built a new King's bedchamber, in addition to his grandfather's Painted Chamber which had, with the passage of time, become too much of a public meeting place for the court in general. The new more private King's bedroom was called the White Chamber, but little is known of its architectural character.

By the reign of Edward II Westminster Palace had become clearly differentiated into two parts – the Great Palace and the Privy Palace. The Great Palace occupied the east and oldest part of the site and comprised the official government departments, such as the law courts and the Exchequer, established in the purlieus of Westminster Hall. The Privy Palace occupied the area to the west of St Stephen's Chapel and was reserved for the occupation of the royal family. It comprised the Lesser Hall, the Painted Chamber, the Queen's Apartments, the Green Chamber, the new White Chamber, accommodation for favourites and household staff, and the gardens. Within its precincts was a separate self-contained residence for the King's eldest son, called the Prince's Palace. All these buildings were two-storeyed and of stone. The layout was

Sala Regalis cum Curia Wett monastery, vulgo Wettminster haall.

Palace of Westminster. Engraving of New Palace Yard by Wenceslas Hollar showing Westminster Hall, the conduit and Edward III's Clock Tower.

surrounded by a wall except on the Thames side, where the river was white with the royal swans who were kept there and plucked once a year to make feather beds for the palace.[3]

Edward II's favourite country house was King's Langley in Hertfordshire, where he had done much building in the 1290s before he succeeded to the throne. This palace has been completely demolished, but the site was excavated in 1970 and a little information discovered about the original layout. It comprised at least two courtyards, one a kitchen court with a six-bay wine cellar, bakehouse, kitchen and so forth. Nothing is known of the treatment of the royal apartments. King's Langley had come to the Crown by escheat when its owner died intestate in 1274 and had been granted to Edward for his own occupation when still Prince of Wales. Edward's building work was prematurely cut short by his deposition and murder at Berkeley Castle, leaving his terrible wife, the 'She-wolf of France', and her lover Mortimer in control, till Edward III came of age and locked his mother safely away in Framlingham Castle. The effective rule of Edward III inaugurated a period of large-scale improvements and additions to the royal residences only equalled by the achievement of Henry III. Considerable sums were spent on many of the older royal houses and castles such as Clarendon, Woodstock, Havering and Gloucester. Four new hunting lodges were constructed in the New Forest, and two major new palaces – Sheen and Eltham – initiated.

Sheen had come to the Crown under Edward II. Between 1358 and 1370 Edward III spent £2,000 on a series of new buildings including a great gatehouse, houses for courtiers, and royal apartments including a King's Chamber with two fireplaces and an elaborately wrought candelabra of 'fine flowers in the form of roses'. In the last twenty years of his life Sheen became one of that select group of comfortable royal residences in the home counties where Edward III increasingly spent his time. His other major new house was Eltham on the other side of London. It had been left to Edward II by Bishop Bek of Durham in 1311. Edward III carried out various improvements, including a new gatehouse

Palace of Westminster. The Jewel Tower built by Edward III.

and a set of royal apartments, and spent much time there. In October 1347 he held a splendid tournament at Eltham Palace to celebrate his victories over France and his own safe return together with that of the Black Prince.

At Westminster between 1331 and 1363 Edward III spent £29,000. He reconstructed the King's Bathroom, installing a new bath with running hot and cold water and bronze taps, and rebuilt the Great Conduit in the Privy Palace. He built a belfry in the middle of the south side of Westminster Hall with a large bell, 'Edward of Westminster', weighing 9,261 lbs, and erected the tall Clock Tower in the Outer Yard as well as the Jewel Tower at the north-west corner of the Privy Palace, which still exists. He also redecorated some of the rooms and created the *Chambre des Étoiles* – the Star Chamber – called after its decoration. His major achievement at Westminster, however, was the completion of St Stephen's Chapel. The lavish decoration of the upper chapel took fourteen or fifteen years to execute and included stained glass windows, gilded statues, carved screens, and one of the most elaborate schemes of wall painting ever carried out in England. The whole surface of the walls and the timber vaulted roof was diapered and stencilled in gold, silver, red, blue, green and yellow, while round the lower parts of the walls beneath the windows were

Top: Palace of
Westminster. St Stephen's
Chapel, section showing
the upper part before it
was burnt in 1834.

Above: Palace of
Westminster. St Stephen's
Chapel. Detail of wall
paintings (destroyed in
1801).

Palace of Westminster. St
Stephen's Cloisters,
exterior.

eighty panels of religious subjects. The altar and paving were of Purbeck marble and there were elaborately carved wooden stalls for the canons who served the chapel. Between the windows were sumptuous canopied niches with carved stone angels holding real thuribles of gilt metal. The whole formed one of the earliest and most perfect examples of Perpendicular architecture in the country. The exterior was equally majestic, riding high above the other palace buildings, with its steep-pitched roof, four corner turrets, and huge traceried east window. It survived relatively unscathed until secularization in 1548, when it became the House of Commons and its architectural character was progressively obliterated. The wall paintings were whitewashed over, and finally destroyed in the early nineteenth century to make way for benches for Irish MPs, following the Act of Union in 1801. The remains of the upper chapel were burnt in 1834, and today only the lower chapel, dedicated to St Mary, survives, as restored in the 1860s by Sir Charles Barry and Son.[4]

Edward III's most important palace-building project was his reconstruction of Windsor Castle, perhaps the most ambitious single architectural scheme in the history of the English royal residences. The major burst of activity took place in the 1350s, following the great victories over the French at Crécy and Poitiers, the capture of Calais, and the imposition of independent English sovereignty over Aquitaine and Gascony (which had formerly been held as fiefs

Windsor Castle. Bird's eye view by Wenceslas Hollar showing the royal apartments in the Upper Ward after rebuilding by Edward III.

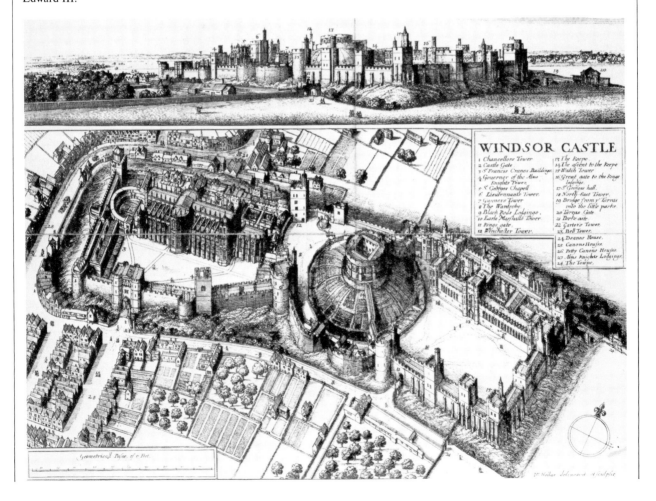

Windsor Castle. The North side.

from the French Crown). It was above all at Windsor that Edward III rivalled Henry III as a patron of architecture. He spent more on converting the castle into a splendid fortified palace, redolent of chivalry and military glory, than any other medieval English king spent on any other single building. Windsor was the intended centre of his court and chivalry, and the seat of the newly-founded Order of the Garter. It expressed Edward III's conception of kingship as surely as Versailles that of Louis XIV or the Vatican that of the papacy. It was an expression of strong personal monarchy and military glory. As he grew older, and he reigned for over fifty years, Edward spent less time at Westminster and more at Windsor and the other country houses in the Thames Valley, while the 'hunting lodge' which Henry III had built in Windsor Great Park became Edward's favourite retreat from the cares of state, rather in the way that Osborne was Queen Victoria's. After 1372 the chief officers of the household were based permanently at Windsor. When the King moved to his lesser houses, he was no longer accompanied by his full household but just by his personal attendants, forming a smaller 'riding household', and this pattern survived for the remainder of the Middle Ages.

Edward III's work at Windsor began in 1350 and falls into two phases – work in the Lower Ward consequent on the founding of the Order of the Garter, and work in the Upper Ward where a new palace was constructed round two cloister courts on the north side of the quadrangle. The alterations to the Lower Ward were designed to provide accommodation for the priestly College of St George, founded on 6 August 1348. It comprised a dean, twelve canons and thirteen vicars-choral. In addition, there were twenty-six Poor Knights, who were to attend Mass daily as a substitute for the Companions of the Order who were too busy elsewhere. Henry III's handsome chapel was made over to the Order and re-named St George's Chapel. Henry's royal lodgings in the Lower Ward were transformed into accommodation for the clergy and a new cloister built, with traceried Perpendicular windows and a massive beamed ceiling, as well as a treasury and chapter house. A mechanical weight-driven clock, the earliest recorded in England, was set up in the Round Tower at the same time. These various works, which cost £6,500, were completed by 1358, and to mark the

Windsor Castle

■ Henry II

▨ Henry III

▢ Edward III

▥ Henry V and Henry VI

■ Edward IV and Tudor

1 *Clewer Tower*
2 *Vicars' Lodgings*
3 *Garters Tower*
4 *Salisbury Tower*
5 *Henry VIII's Gate*
6 *Site of Great Hall*
7 *St George's Chapel*
8 *Tower Ward*
9 *Lodgings of the Military Knights*
10 *Cloisters*
11 *Lady Chapel*
12 *Winchester Tower*
13 *Henry III's Tower*

occasion the Feast of St George was celebrated by the King and court with great splendour at the castle in that year.

The reconstruction of the Upper Ward, begun in 1357, was on a larger scale than the work in the Lower Ward. The new royal lodgings were constructed of stone under the direction of William of Wykeham. An inner gatehouse flanked by two cylindrical towers was built to give access to the Upper Ward from the Lower in 1359. It still survives, albeit restored, but is now misleadingly called the 'Norman Gate'. Only some of the masonry of the present state apartments and the handsome vaulted undercroft survives of Edward III's royal lodgings, but the original accounts, together with the engravings of Windsor by Wenceslas Hollar in Elias Ashmole's seventeenth-century *History of the Most Noble Order of the Garter*, give some impression. The major new apartments were on the first floor, in accordance with the traditional arrangement of the English royal residences; they were raised over vaulted undercrofts, the stone ribbed ceilings of which were supported on slender octagonal piers. The principal rooms were grouped around two courtyards, later known as the Brick Court and the Horn Court, with two-tier cloisters and paving of Purbeck marble. The King's apartment consisted of five chambers and a closet. The other principal rooms

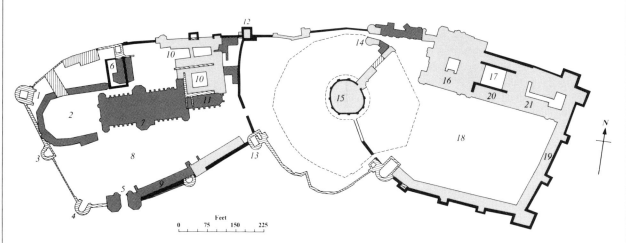

14 *Inner Gateway*
15 *Round Tower*
16 *State Apartments*
17 *Horn Court*
18 *Upper Ward*
19 *Lodgings*
20 *Chapel*
21 *St George's Hall*

included a Great Chamber and a Painted Chamber. Along the south side, facing into the quadrangle of the Upper Ward, were the Great Hall and Private Chapel, end to end, an identical arrangement to that surviving at William of Wykeham's New College, Oxford. The appearance of the chapel is not known, but the hall had an open timber roof decorated with carved tracery. By his death in 1377, Edward III had spent £50,772 on Windsor Castle. But of his work, the only parts which survive as visually coherent pieces of architecture are the cloisters of St George's Chapel, the Inner Gateway, and the undercroft of the state apartments. Everything else was disguised and altered in the reconstruction of the seventeenth and nineteenth centuries. The existing St

Windsor Castle. St George's Hall, engraved by Wenceslas Hollar.

George's Hall, for example, comprises both Edward III's chapel and hall knocked together to form one disproportionately long room.[5] Nevertheless Windsor retains the pre-eminence among the royal residences of England which Edward III's reconstruction gave it, and is the only one of the medieval palaces to have been, more or less, continuously inhabited down to the present day.[5]

Richard II, the son of the Black Prince, who succeeded his grandfather in 1377, was a complete contrast to both. He was neither a warrior nor an astute politician and failed signally to get on with the barons. He was notorious for his pompous court ceremony, with a great deal of crown wearing and emphasis on the majesty of the monarch. People were expected to bend their knee to him and to recognize the sacred character of their anointed sovereign. He began the process which led to the royal household becoming a great deal more formal in an effort to outshine the splendour of the great aristocratic households. Richard II was also the royal aesthete *par excellence*, a lover of beauty, books, exotic cooking, extravagant clothes, as well as being the inventor of the pocket handkerchief.

Westminster was of special interest to him because of his personal cult of Edward the Confessor, whom he adopted as his patron saint. He carried out several further improvements and embellishments under the direction of the celebrated Master Mason, Henry Yevele. A new Great Gateway was built into the Outer Yard before Westminster Hall, and the bath tub in the King's apartments at the Privy Palace was once again remade and provided with new bronze taps for hot and cold water. The supreme work of the reign, however,

Westminster Hall as refronted by Richard II in 1394–1401.

Westminster Hall. Interior showing the hammerbeam roof erected by Hugh Herland for Richard II.

was the reconstruction of Westminster Hall between 1394 and 1401. The walls were heightened and refaced under Yevele's direction. Sturdy flying buttresses were added to support the new single span timber roof and, as part of the decoration of the hall, a series of carved stone statues was set up, showing the English kings from Edward the Confessor onwards, a unique historical sculpture gallery. The chief glory of the re-edified hall was the timber roof constructed by Hugh Herland. It was the first hammerbeam roof ever to be built, and with a span of 69 feet, was the largest timber roof in northern Europe. It survives as the greatest masterpiece of English medieval carpentry, its beams carved with angels and traceried patterns. No other remnant of the English medieval royal residences gives such a good idea of the grandeur of their scale and the splendour and originality of their design. It is one of the ironies of history that this magnificent room should have been used first for Richard II's deposition ceremony. In Richard's reign Westminster Palace finally reached the form it retained for the remainder of its existence as a royal residence, and, apart from the fan-vaulted cloisters of St Stephen's Chapel added by Henry VII, no further important work was undertaken there in the ensuing hundred years.[6]

Richard II's favourite palace was Sheen in Surrey. It was one of the select new group of royal residences in the Thames Valley favoured by Edward III, and he had in fact died there on 21 June 1377. Richard carried on the improvements begun by his grandfather and built a magnificent new bathroom, the walls of which were lined with 2,000 painted tiles. His most striking innovation was a little summer house intended for quiet retirement, the first recorded in English architecture. This retreat was built on an adjoining island in the River Thames and was timber-framed on a stone foundation and equipped with benches and a table. On the death at Sheen of his consort Queen Anne of Bohemia on 7 June 1394, Richard with a morbidly romantic gesture ordered the palace to be demolished and the site left desolate.

The deposition of Richard II and succession to the throne of the Lancastrian dynasty in the person of Henry IV caused no drastic alteration in the distribution or character of the royal residences. In his short reign Henry IV continued the architectural policies of his predecessors and, for example, enlarged the existing buildings at Eltham. His son, Henry V, the greatest of the Lancastrian kings, decided to rebuild Sheen as the architectural embodiment of the new dynasty and to make it once more one of the principal royal houses of the kingdom. Work began in 1414 and continued until his death, but then languished and the enterprise was never completed. The new buildings at Sheen were of red brick, the first time that this material had been used on a large scale in a royal palace. This choice reflected the sudden fashion for brick inspired by the brick castles and churches of the Low Countries and northern France which the English had seen and admired on their victorious campaigns. The new palace of Sheen was a celebration of Henry V's victories in France, much as Edward III's Windsor had been the expression of his. Sheen was paid for out of the King's substantial war profits following Agincourt, Harfleur and the conquest of Paris. The layout was appropriately grand. The main quadrangle was approximately 175 feet by 208 feet. The Great Hall was 77 feet long and 40 feet wide. The chapel was on the same scale and supported on a vaulted undercroft. The details of Henry V's works at Sheen are not known because his unfinished buildings were destroyed by fire in 1499 and replaced by Henry VII to a different design.

The reign of Henry V saw the power of the medieval English Crown reach its widest extent with the conquest of the richest part of France. This triumph was short-lived. The King's premature death, a long minority and then the feeble personal rule of Henry VI saw the ignominious defeat of England, the loss of all the Crown's continental possessions except for Calais, and the breakdown of the royal administration in England itself. This series of catastrophes was marked by a hiatus in royal palace-building in England, though Henry VI did embark on a series of important religious and collegiate works. In 1461 he was deposed and replaced by the Yorkist Edward IV. At first Edward was too insecure to pay much attention to his residences, but following the abortive restoration, defeat and death of Henry VI in 1471, Edward was able to demonstrate his newly acquired confidence by embarking on a programme of building work. This was made financially possible by the secret pension he obtained from Louis XI at the Treaty of Picquigny as a bribe for abandoning the Burgundians. He intended to make Eltham a Yorkist answer to the Lancastrian Sheen, and extensive works were put in hand there between 1479 and 1482 under the direction of James Hatefelde. Edward's principal achievement at Eltham, and apart from the bridge over the moat the only part of the medieval palace to survive, was the noble Great Hall. It was first used for Christmas 1482, when 2,000 people were entertained with great magnificence. It is a secular Gothic masterpiece, with an excellently designed timber hammerbeam roof and large traceried windows, the bay windows lighting the dais at the high table and having pretty little stone vaults. These windows were originally fitted with a resplendent display of the Yorkist heraldry in stained glass. The lower parts of the walls were hung with tapestry, a fashion that had superseded the earlier

Eltham Palace. Exterior of the remaining buildings and the moat. The Great Hall built by Edward IV was completed in 1482.

Eltham Palace. Fifteenth century bridge over the moat.

medieval taste for painted decoration in the course of the fifteenth century. As early as 1468 Edward had bought a set of four large pieces of tapestry showing classical and religious scenes – the stories of Nebuchadnezzar and Alexander, the Passion and Last Judgment. Another development in the fifteenth century was the emergence of regular quadrangular planning in place of the haphazard accretions of the thirteenth and fourteenth-century palaces, and the development of a standard sequence of state rooms out of the old Great Chamber. Both these developments were to come to fruition in the following century.

The hall at Eltham was eclipsed by Edward IV's other major architectural project – the rebuilding of St George's Chapel at Windsor – begun in 1473. The old buildings to the west of Henry III's chapel (which itself was demolished and replaced by Henry VII) were cleared away to make a site for a large new Perpendicular chapel of cruciform plan with nave, transepts and choir rather like a large town-parish church. It was intended to have a tower over the central crossing, but this was omitted when the chapel was completed, after Edward's death and the overthrow of Richard III, by Henry VII, who gave the whole chapel a continuous stone vault. Edward IV's St George's Chapel is one of the great monuments of English Gothic architecture and the grandest surviving English medieval palace chapel. It was constructed under the direction of the mason Henry Janyns, but at the time of Edward's death, only the choir had been roofed. The work at St George's also included the semi-circular layout of brick and timber-framed houses for the vicars-choral at the west end of the chapel, which survive, heavily restored, and are now called the Horseshoe Cloisters.[7]

As well as his architectural work, Edward IV made a great effort to restore dignity and order to the royal household, following the shabby chaos of Henry

Windsor. St George's
Chapel, begun by Edward
IV and completed under
Henry VII. It is the
grandest of the medieval
royal chapels to survive.

Windsor. St George's
Cloisters as rebuilt by
Edward IV but
incorporating some of the
fabric of Henry III's.

VI's reign. A new formality was introduced on the model of the court of Edward's brother-in-law, Charles the Bold of Burgundy, whose day-to-day ceremonial was the grandest in Europe. Edward's emulation of the ducal court at Dijon included purchasing Burgundian tapestries and illuminated manuscripts. The Burgundian Master of Ceremonies, Olivier de la Marche, was consulted over details of household management and the ritual to be observed at state banquets; his celebrated treatise, *L'État de la Maison du Duc Charles de Burgonyne dict Le Hardy* was written in 1473–4 in response to queries about etiquette from the English court. This attempt to regularize the royal household and to make it more dignified also prompted the compilation of the Black Book of the Household, which laid down regulations governing different aspects of the royal household, above and below stairs. Edward's reforms also introduced a necessary degree of careful economy into the running of the household, which comprised about 1,400 officials in the fifteenth century. Edward made a successful attempt to curtail extravagance and was able to cut down annual expenditure to £12,000. He was the first king since Henry II to die not in debt. In all this he foreshadowed the policies of the Tudors.[8]

III

THE TUDORS

The early sixteenth century is one of the most rewarding periods in the history of English royal building activity. The second half of the century, on the other hand, is almost entirely fallow. Edward VI and Mary did nothing, while Elizabeth restricted her building expenditure to routine repairs and minor additions. But both the first two Tudors were great builders. Between 1494 and 1509 Henry VII spent at least £28,000 on his principal houses – building on a large scale at Richmond and Greenwich and making substantial alterations at Windsor, Woodstock and elsewhere. In addition to his palaces, he was also engaged on a series of religious building works. At Windsor he added a new mortuary chapel, or Tomb House, behind St George's with the intention of placing there his own monument together with that of Henry VI. This project was diverted to Westminster Abbey when the abbot of that establishment, unsuccessfully, claimed possession of the body of Henry VI, and this resulted in the construction of the Henry VII Chapel there.

Henry VIII, by contrast, was responsible for work of an almost exclusively secular character. In the early years of his reign, between 1515 and 1522, he built two new houses at a cost of £39,000 – Bridewell in London (converted into a prison by Edward VI) and Beaulieu or New Hall in Essex (later in the sixteenth century alienated from the Crown to become a private house of the Earls of Sussex). Both these houses were quadrangular and of traditional character. It was only on the downfall of Wolsey in 1529 that Henry VIII revealed himself as one of the greatest of all royal builders. In the last two decades of his reign by exchange, forfeiture and purchase he acquired house after house in the counties round London, and by the time of his death he had amassed over forty houses, the high water-mark of the English royal residences. At Whitehall and Hampton Court, both confiscated from Wolsey, he continued the Cardinal's work on an even more ambitious scale. At Windsor he made new state apartments and a new entrance gateway. At Oatlands and St James's he built completely new palaces in the late medieval style and at Nonsuch erected a major new palace with Renaissance decoration. Building on this scale was a strain on both the royal finances and the royal administration. 'What a gret charge it is to (his) highness to contineu his byldings in so many placys at oons', wrote Thomas Cromwell in 1534.[1]

The palaces of Henry VII and Henry VIII were intended as a visible expression of the new dynasty and formed an important instrument of Tudor policy. Henry VII, though generally careful with money, 'never spared charge which his affairs required, and in his building he was magnificent'. His major new palace, and the earliest assertion of the glory of the Tudor dynasty, was Richmond in Surrey. In 1497 the old palace of Sheen had burnt down. Henry VII immediately decided to replace it, and re-named it Richmond by way of perpetuating the name of his former earldom. The new palace covered ten acres and had a regular layout round a series of spacious courtyards. The main axis formed a succession of three courts. The outer, called the Wardrobe Court, was surrounded by two-storeyed buildings of brick containing the lodgings for the royal household. The Middle Court was flanked by the more-or-less symmetrical hall and chapel like 'stately twins' built of stone. The third quadrangle, containing the royal quarters, was the principal feature of the palace. It was taller than the rest, built of stone, and accentuated by fourteen towers with onion cupolas 'which very much adorn and set forth the whole fabric and are a very graceful ornament to the whole house' and 'upon each of them (was) a vane of the King's arms painted and gilt with rich gold and azure'. On either side of the main courts were three or four subsidiary courts of brick or half-timber containing extensive offices – wood-yards, slaughter-houses, stabling and so forth. The livery kitchen formed an almost independent structure with a tall conical roof in the medieval manner, and near the river was a large 'house of office'.

Richmond Palace. Drawing by Wenceslas Hollar 1638.

Richmond was an ornate Perpendicular palace free from Renaissance influence in its details but showing awareness of new attitudes in the regularity and symmetry of its layout. Its principal attraction, however, the romantic skyline with turrets and gilded weather-vanes, was purely medieval. The palace was well situated between Richmond Green and the River Thames and was flanked by gardens and orchards 'all planted with cherry trees and other fruits to the number of two hundred and twenty-two trees'. In the orchard was a large aviary called the 'Turtle Cage'. Richmond Green itself covered twenty acres and was neatly turfed and planted with elm trees and had 'a very handsome walk' along either side. There was a piped water supply from the start, two systems of elm pipes being laid in 1498, one tapping springs in the park and one in Richmond fields, to feed the White and Red conduits and the fountain in the central quadrangle of the royal lodgings. This latter was a major ornament of the palace. 'In the upper part there are lions and red dragons and other goodly beasts, and in the midst certain branches of red roses, out of which flowers and roses is evermore running an course of clear and most purest water into the cistern beneath. This conduit profitably serves the chambers with water for the hands, and other offices as they need to resort.'[2]

The extensive outbuildings included eighteen kitchens to cook food for the vast household which swamped the building when the court was in residence. Pedro Enriquez, who accompanied Philip II of Spain to England on his nuptial visit in the mid-sixteenth century, recorded his impression when Philip and Mary spent part of their honeymoon at Richmond:

Notwithstanding the greatness of these palaces – and the smallest of the four we have been in has more rooms and better than the Alcazar of Madrid – the crowds in them are so great as to be hardly contained.

He went on to say:

The ordinary consumption of the Palace is from eighty to a hundred sheep with a dozen fat oxen and a dozen and a half of calves, besides vast quantities of game, poultry, venison, wild boar and rabbits, whilst in beer they drink more in summer than the river would hold at Valladolid.

The two principal rooms at Richmond were the hall and the chapel, each a hundred feet long and about forty feet across. The hall had an elaborate timber roof with hanging pendants and 'proper knots craftily carved . . . after the most new invention'. There was a lantern in the roof over a central charcoal fire. The upper parts of the walls had large Perpendicular windows with paintings in between of those kings of England who were renowned in battle including Hengist, William the Conqueror, Richard I and Henry VII himself (as victor of Bosworth), all 'appearing like bold and valiant knights'. Below were statues and tapestries. The 'whole apartment was glorious and joyful to behold'. The chapel was even more richly appointed. The walls were hung with cloth of gold and the altars 'set with many relics, jewels and full rich play'. Between the windows, as a pendant to the scheme in the hall, were paintings of those English kings 'whose life and virtue was so abundant that it hath pleased Almighty God to show by the diverse and many miracles, and to be reckoned as Saints', such as Edward the Confessor, St Edmund, and Cadwallader. The many fittings included 'handsome Cathedral pews, a removable pulpit and a fair case of carved work for a pair of organs'. The latter recalls one of the principal glories of the sixteenth-century English palaces, the magnificent music of the royal chapels. Niccolo Sagulino, who heard Mass at Richmond in 1515, found the voices of the choristers 'more divine than human – and as to the counter-bass voices they probably have not equals in the world'. It was royal patronage that was largely responsible for that musical culture which flourished throughout the century and was second only to that of Renaissance Italy.

The principal quadrangle had twelve rooms on each floor as well as a succession of 'goodly passages and galleries, paved, glazed and painted, beset with badges of gold, as roses, portcullises and such others'. The main sequence of state apartments leading out of the Great Hall comprised the Guard Chamber, Presence Chamber, Privy Chamber, King's Bedchamber and the closet, all 'hanged with rich and costly cloth of Arras, ceiled, white limed and checkered . . . with their goodly bay windows glazed . . .'[3] Tapestry had replaced the early medieval fashion for painted decoration by the early sixteenth century. Such hangings were only left in position when the court was in residence, otherwise they were kept in store and the walls left bare. Many different sets were acquired so that they could be changed according to the seasons. In some English palaces they were changed as often as once a week, partly out of regal ostentation and partly for practical reasons, to stop the colours fading by too long exposure to the light.

Henry VII's other great new palace, Greenwich, lacked the overall regularity of Richmond, for there he was enlarging and remodelling an existing building and not starting out anew. It had been begun by Humphry, Duke of Gloucester, Henry V's younger brother and Regent during the minority of Henry VI, and was called by him Bella Vista. Duke Humphry was a dissolute but cultivated man and one of the first English patrons of the 'new learning'. He formed a great library filled with the works of Plato, Aristotle, Virgil, Dante, Petrarch, Boccaccio, which he left to Oxford as the nucleus of the Bodleian Library. His love of scholarship was combined with vaunting political ambition, and he was eventually arrested for 'High Treason' and died mysteriously in the Tower. Greenwich was taken over by Henry VI's domineering French wife, Margaret of Anjou, who changed its name to Placentia and spent a great deal of money embellishing everything with carved daisies, a pun on her heraldry. Later Edward IV gave it to his queen, Elizabeth Woodville. Under Henry VII it became one of the major English royal palaces, a position it held till the early seventeenth century. Henry modernized it and faced it in red brick. The centre of the layout was a courtyard 100 feet square, with straggling wings forming lesser courts on either side and prolonging the main front, which was directly alongside the river, to 500 feet. The chapel was at the east end and a grand

Greenwich Palace from the River Thames. Drawing by Anthony van Wyngaerde.

gatehouse was situated near the middle of the front range, forming the main entrance from the water. The chief buildings were two-storeyed, with crenellated parapets, octangular towers, and steeply pitched roofs. The overall impression was of a long, low, sprawling layout in contrast to the taller more compact design of Richmond. The exact disposition of the buildings is not known, and modern excavations have shown that the views of the palace by Anthony van Wyngaerde in the mid-sixteenth century and by Wenceslas Hollar in the early seventeenth century were not strictly accurate.[4]

Henry VIII, who was born and brought up at Greenwich, was especially fond of it, and carried out many embellishments as well as installing his famous armouries there and founding the royal dockyards nearby at Deptford and Woolwich. In the Fountain Court he erected a large conduit of Renaissance design with cornices, columns and spheres 'painted in a fine jasper colour' and enriched with heraldry and 'carved antique work'. He also spent a fortune on the gardens, which he made into some of the finest in Europe, laying out a tiltyard and an elaborate privy garden on the landward side between the palace and the park. Special features introduced by him were a 'water maze' and a coop of peacocks 'brought to the King out of the new-found land'. The latter, however, were soon removed because 'the Queen's Grace could not take her rest in the morning for the noise of the same'. Henry also carried out ambitious schemes of decoration in the Renaissance taste, employing at Greenwich the greatest of the foreign artists whom he was able to lure to England, the German Hans Holbein. A great deal of work was done specially for the reception of the French ambassador in 1527. Two temporary halls, decorated by Holbein (on his first visit to England) and a team of painters, were erected in the tiltyard, one for use as an 'amphitheatre' and the other as a banqueting house. Two timber 'arches triumphant antique wise' were constructed at a cost of £262 9s 8d, one as the screen in the hall where supper was served, and the other as a backdrop to the throne in the hall where entertainments were given after the feast. The latter also had a ceiling painted with a map of the world. Spinelli, the Venetian ambassador who was present at this magnificent reception, wrote: 'One thing above all surprised me, never having witnessed the like anywhere, it being impossible to represent or credit with how much order, regularity and silence such public entertainments are conducted in England.'[5]

Hans Holbein, who settled in London permanently in 1532, was only one of a series of foreign artists and craftsmen with experience of Italian art and architectural decoration whom Henry VIII invited into England. His court saw the first flowering of Italian Renaissance design in this country and produced work comparable with the contemporary achievements of Francis I in France and Charles V in Spain. Henry's patronage of the arts was as much an act of conscious rivalry with his richer and more powerful brother monarchs as was his over-ambitious foreign and military policy. The most famous of the Italian artists he employed were Pietro Torrigiano, who made the beautiful bronze royal tombs in Henry VII's Chapel at Westminster Abbey, and Giovanni da Majano, who made the terracotta roundels of Roman emperors to embellish the gatehouses at Whitehall and Hampton Court. Others less well known were Antonio Toto, who became Henry VIII's Sergeant-Painter, Nicholas Lizard, and Nicholas Bellin of Modena, who had previously worked for Francis I at Fontainebleau but being charged with fraud escaped to England. Bellin designed a timber banqueting house at Whitehall and was responsible for the slate and stucco decorations of Nonsuch. The Italianate preaching place or open-air pulpit at Whitehall was also designed by him and built by Robert Trunchey under his direction. John of 'Padoa', described in the accounts as an 'architect', is a more shadowy character. He was a versatile artist and a talented musician, but it is not entirely clear what he did in the royal palaces because most of Henry's interior work has disappeared without record. Giovanni Portinari was employed by Henry to complete Benedetto da Rovezzano's monument to Wolsey which the King confiscated at the time of the Cardinal's fall. Its appearance when finished is not known, because all the bronzework was destroyed or dispersed during the Civil War in 1646 and only the black marble sarcophagus survives as the burial place of Lord Nelson in the crypt of St Paul's Cathedral. Henry VIII's 'court school' is an interesting episode in English art history, but too little survives to form a clear impression of what was achieved. The early sixteenth-century royal palaces were hybrids with pure Renaissance decoration and features grafted on to architectural forms of traditional Gothic character.[6] In the later years of Henry's reign this Renaissance influence seems to have come to England via France rather than directly from Italy, as had at first been the case. The decoration at Whitehall, Nonsuch and elsewhere, for instance, owed more to Francis I's School of Fontainebleau than to anything in contemporary Rome or Florence.

Though an active builder from the earliest years of his reign, Henry VIII only came into his own with the fall of Wolsey. The latter's two palaces of Hampton Court and York Place (soon to be unofficially re-named Whitehall) were taken over by the King, though technically York Place was not Wolsey's personal property but the official London residence of the Archbishop of York. Wolsey had already enlarged it 'sumptuously and gloriously', but this was merely an overture to Henry's far more ambitious scheme. He made Whitehall the principal royal residence in London. The Palace of Westminster, which was

Whitehall Palace. Bird's-eye view by Anthony van Wyngaerde.

Top: Whitehall Palace from St James's Park showing the cockpit and tennis court.

Above: Whitehall Palace. The wine cellar which is still preserved under the Ministry of Defence.

beginning to seem old-fashioned and down at heel, was handed over entirely to the central government bureaucracy. The King did not wait for the completion of legal formalities before taking possession of York Place. On 2 November 1529, only a few days after Wolsey's departure, he came from Greenwich by water in the gilded royal barge with its cloth of gold hangings and 'landed at the house which once belonged to the Cardinal where he found handsome and well-furnished apartments provided with everything that could be wished'.[7] Henry was determined that Whitehall should be a new royal residence which would eclipse Westminster in every way. He enlarged its curtilage by acquiring land from Westminster Abbey and from Eton. The latter gave up the Hospital of St James which Henry demolished and rebuilt as a subsidiary palace, making the ground between it and York Place into a new park. Wolsey's palace had occupied the land east of the present line of Whitehall, roughly between the Banqueting House and the river. Henry doubled the size of the palace by building a whole series of new buildings on the west side of the street facing the new park. On the land acquired from Westminster Abbey, south along the river between York Place and Lamb Alley, he laid out an orchard (later the Privy Garden). The new west extension comprised buildings intended chiefly for recreational purposes: the octagonal cockpit, tennis courts, a bowling alley, pheasant yard and a tiltyard. The site of the latter is occupied approximately by the present Horse Guards. Access to this west extension from the old part of the palace was by two new gatehouses spanning the public street from Westminster to Charing

Left: Whitehall Palace. The 'Holbein Gate' decorated with terracotta roundels of Roman emperors.

Right: Whitehall Palace. The King Street Gate.

Cross: the north gatehouse (later called for no sound reason the 'Holbein Gate'), and the south gate (later called the King Street Gate). The King's Gate had a vaulted archway and angle turrets similar to the contemporary college gates at Oxford or Cambridge, but was decorated with roundels of Roman emperors. The south gate was the purest piece of French-style Renaissance architecture at that time in England, embellished with tiers of Doric and Ionic pilasters and with little pediments over the side-entrances, and little cupolas on top.

The King's new building operations were begun immediately after acquiring the leasehold interests in the Westminster Abbey property. In April 1531 the ambassador from Milan wrote: 'His Majesty is now staying at Greenwich, and comes often to Westminster, having designed new lodgings there and a park adjoining York House which belonged to the late Cardinal Wolsey. The place is on so large a scale that many hundreds of houses will be levelled nearly all of which belong to great personages.'[8] Some of the existing palace, as well as neighbouring houses, was demolished, but the central part of Wolsey's premises with its courtyard, new-built hall, wine-cellar and chapel was retained as the nucleus of Henry VIII's palace. The King seems to have gone out of his way to slight Wolsey's memory. The Cardinal's new college at Ipswich, for instance, was abolished and the stone brought to Whitehall to be used there, while the timber gallery at Wolsey's house at Esher was dismantled and re-erected as the Privy Gallery at Whitehall.

Henry VIII's Whitehall was the largest palace in Europe and covered about twenty-three acres, but it did not have any overall form or regular layout. It was a loose assemblage of different courts, gardens and buildings with a public street down the middle, but linked by a straggling network of galleries, several of them placed one over the other. These galleries, which formed the chief means of communication between the different parts of the palace, were a novelty in English domestic planning and set the fashion for long galleries in later sixteenth-century houses. The most striking was the Privy Gallery, which continued the passage over the 'Holbein Gate' and the axis of the Tiltyard Gallery on the west side of the street and thus formed the principal communication along the north side of the palace between the King's privy lodgings at the east and St James's Park on the west. There were at least five other galleries. The Low Gallery also ran east–west, while the Stone Gallery ran at right-angles to the Privy Gallery. Its walls were decorated with paintings of the 'Coronacion of our saide Sovereign Lorde'. Above it was the Matted Gallery, the principal long gallery of the palace. It was embellished with an especially elaborate Renaissance plaster ceiling with panels, 'pilasters', rich mouldings and, according to Evelyn, paintings by Holbein.[9] Another gallery called the Shield Gallery was hung with the shields presented at tournaments in the tiltyard.

The principal court, or Great Court, was also sometimes called Whalebone Court after 'the monstrous great whale's bone' displayed there. From it a covered passage ran at right-angles towards the Great Hall, the Chapel Royal, and the Water Gate or Whitehall Stairs on the Thames. The Great Hall was erected by Wolsey in 1528; it was of standard plan, with six windows along the sides and large bays at the dais end. The interior had a stone-paved floor covered with mats of rushes and an open timber roof with a central louvre. The exterior was stone-faced and had a battlemented parapet. To the east was the Chapel Royal, 75 feet long and 28 feet wide. It had large traceried windows with stained glass and wainscotting painted with religious subjects round the lower parts of the walls. On the battlements stood carved figures on high plinths. The King's pew was in a gallery over the passage leading to the Water Gate.

Whitehall Palace. Cartoon by Holbein for part of the mural of the Tudor dynasty in the Privy Chamber.

North of the Great Court was Henry VIII's Privy Garden (later called the Sermon Court or Pebble Court and not to be confused with the orchard on the south side of the palace which became the Privy Garden in the seventeenth century). Here was situated the open-air pulpit designed by Nicholas Bellin in which Latimer preached before Edward VI. The Bohemian emissary Von Wedel described its appearance in 1584: 'Then we were brought to a grass plot surrounded by broad walks below and above, enabling many persons to promenade there. In the middle of the place a pulpit is erected with a sounding board above. When the Queen commands preaching here, the walks are filled with auditors.'[10] Along the north and east sides were balustraded wooden terraces on square piers, giving access to the Privy Lodgings and the Council Chamber. They were sometimes used for purposes other than listening to sermons. In 1604, for instance, it was noted that 'one woeman among the rest lost her honesty, for wch she was caried to the porter's lodge, being surprised at her business on top of the Taras.'[11]

The King's state rooms on the first floor of the Privy Lodgings comprised the Guard Chamber, Presence Chamber and Privy Chamber. Von Wedel described the Presence Chamber as being 'very large and high with gilt ceiling, upon which, on tablets are written the dates of wars that have been made'[12]. The Privy Chamber contained the most famous decoration at Whitehall, the great mural painting of the Tudor dynasty by Holbein, for which the cartoon of Henry VIII himself is preserved in the National Portrait Gallery. (The painting itself

Above: Whitehall Palace. The pulpit designed by Nicholas Bellin.

Top right: Whitehall Palace. Model of the layout in the reign of Henry VIII.

Right: St James's Palace. The Gatehouse.

survived the Civil War but was destroyed in the fire of 1698.) A duplicate set of state apartments for the Queen adjoined the King's and overlooked the river. They were first occupied by Anne Boleyn.

St James's Palace formed an integral part of Henry VIII's programme for Whitehall and was built concurrently in the 1530s. It was intended as a private retreat on the other side of the park where the King could escape from the formalities of his public life. On acquiring the property, he demolished the old hospital buildings (originally intended for maiden lepers) and built a new house with ranges of buildings round four courts – later called Colour Court, Ambassador's Court, Friary Court, and another court to the west. The Tudor buildings were much altered and mutilated in the seventeenth and eighteenth centuries and partly destroyed by fire in 1809, but enough survives to give an approximate impression of Henry VIII's house. It was of red brick with diaper patterns of darker bricks. The principal feature was the gatehouse on the north side, four storeys high, with octagonal corner turrets and a four-centred arch embellished with the initials H.A. for Henry and Anne Boleyn together with a Tudor rose and crown. The chief original interior was the Chapel Royal, 70 feet long and 23 feet wide. The lower parts have been altered but the Tudor ceiling

St James's Palace. The Armoury showing an original fireplace (and the decoration by William Morris).

St James's Palace. The Tapestry Room.

Right: Hampton Court. The Great Gatehouse. This was rebuilt in the reign of George III, but keeping its original form and re-using the roundels of Roman emperors by Giovanni da Majano.

Below: Hampton Court. The base court showing the inner gatehouse and the gable of Henry VIII's Great Hall.

remains, divided by plaster ribs into a series of octagons, cross shapes, and lozenge panels, painted with shields, devices and mottoes including crowned initials HR and the date 1540. One or two smaller rooms, such as the Guard Chamber, retain their original proportions and stone Tudor fireplaces.[13]

Apart from Whitehall Henry VIII also obtained Hampton Court from Wolsey in 1529. There too he continued the Cardinal's work on a grander scale. Wolsey had built Hampton Court on a new site with a regular plan of a progression of courts on a central axis marked by a series of gatehouses. Count Magalotti wrote in 1669 when he visited England with the Grand Duke of Tuscany: 'although the more elegant orders of architecture are not to be found in it, so as to make it a regular structure according to the rules of art, yet it is on the whole a beautiful object to the eye'.[14] So it is, not least because of the fine red brick of the walls and especially elaborate chimneys. Though most of the buildings were only two storeys high, the overall scale was enormous, making it one of the largest houses of its date in Europe. The Base Court was 167 feet by 142 feet and the rest of the palace was on a scale to match. Henry VIII moved in in 1530 and immediately substituted his own arms for Wolsey's everywhere.

Hampton Court. The exterior of Henry VIII's state apartments, Long Gallery and Tennis Court before they were largely demolished to make way for the Wren block.

Hampton Court. The North side showing the kitchen chimneys.

Below left: Hampton Court. Ceiling of the Chapel Royal, with Italian Renaissance decoration.

Bottom left: Hampton Court. The Great Hall.

Below right: Hampton Court. Fan Vault in the bay window of the Great Hall.

Bottom right: Hampton Court. The ceiling of Wolsey's closet, a clue to the rich Tudor Renaissance decoration of the vanished royal apartments.

He built new royal apartments, a new kitchen, tiltyard, a tennis court, and a large new Great Hall. The royal apartments were demolished by William III but the other buildings survive. The vanished apartments had extremely elaborate plaster ceilings and tapestry-hung walls. The chief of them was the Paradise Chamber, a large room hung with jewelled tapestries and with a painted and gilded ceiling. As at Whitehall the architecture at Hampton Court was traditional Perpendicular, but with touches of Renaissance decoration such as the terracotta roundels of Roman emperors in the gatehouses and the carved pendants and spandrels of the hall and chapel ceilings with their Italianate arabesques and cherubs. There were also a number of the fantastic devices much liked by the King, including a huge astronomical clock made by Nicholas Oursian in 1540, which survives and as well as telling the hour, date and month, also gives the number of days since the beginning of the year, the phases of the moon, and the time of high tide at London Bridge.

Interior of Henry VIII's Tennis Court which is still in use.

Hampton Court. Italian terracotta roundel of a Roman Emperor by Giovanni da Majano.

Oatlands Palace. A bird's eye view by Anthony van Wyngaerde.

Just as at Whitehall Henry VIII developed St James's as a subsidiary palace where he could retire from the court, so at Hampton Court he contrived another palace nearby where he could escape to go hunting on his own. This was Oatlands Palace at Weybridge. Henry acquired the property by exchange in 1538 from the Rede family and built a large, rambling brick palace round three or four courts. Only the large square central court aspired to any regularity of architectural form and the royal apartments formed an amorphous, roughly triangular, group of buildings beyond. There seems to have been no Renaissance influence at Oatlands, which was a traditional pile of brick gabled buildings with two large gatehouses with oriel windows and octagonal turrets.[15]

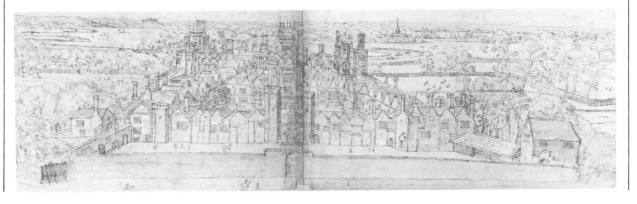

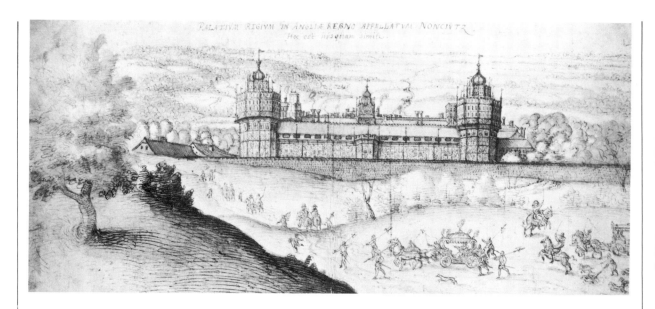

Above: Nonsuch. Drawing **by Hofnagel showing the** arrival of Elizabeth I.

Opposite top: Nonsuch. A cherub's head, part of the stucco decoration executed by Nicholas Bellin.

Opposite below: Nonsuch. A ram's head by Nicholas Bellin.

Henry VIII's extravagant building programme culminated in Nonsuch, his last and favourite palace undertaken in a spirit of conscious rivalry with Francis I and intended as the English Chambord. It cost him nearly £50,000 and 520 workmen were employed on its construction. To make a site, the village and church of Cuddington, ten miles south of London, were cleared away. The suppressed priory of Merton was demolished and its masonry used for the foundations. A deer park of 1,700 acres was created roundabout as a setting for this most elaborate monument to Henry VIII's dynastic and cultural ambitions. Nonsuch comprised two main quadrangles and its overall dimensions were 355 feet by 170 feet with two large octagonal towers at the ends. The outer court contained the domestic offices and was flanked on either side by lesser kitchen and stable courts. This outer court was a comparatively simple two-storeyed affair of stone, completed by the Earl of Arundel to whom Queen Mary gave Nonsuch.[16] The inner court contained the royal apartments and was the *clou* of the palace, a Renaissance fantasy of gilded and painted stuccowork. The inner gatehouse contained an elaborate clock with six 'gilded horoscopes' and a symphony of bells. In the centre of the court was a marble fountain with a horse and the three Graces and opposite the gateway was a statue of Henry VIII sitting under a canopy. The timber-framed walls of the main buildings were covered with a sophisticated veneer of Renaissance decoration, partly engraved slate and partly stucco panels. This was executed by Nicholas Bellin, whom Henry had removed from the service of Francis I in 1537. Camden spoke of 'great . . . emulation of ancient Roman art', and the plaster bas reliefs depicted the Labours of Hercules and other classical, theological and symbolic subjects. Round the upper walls were portraits of thirty-one Roman emperors from Julius Caesar to Aemilianus. Less is known about the interior but it had an interesting plan, without a Great Hall as the palace was intended for the King's 'solace and retirement'. There were no lodgings for courtiers either. The elaborate decoration was no doubt as much influenced by the School of Fontainebleau as was the exterior. There is, for instance, a drawing in the Louvre for the wall decoration of a Privy Chamber in an English royal palace which may be connected with Nonsuch. The gardens were laid out in the formal manner with

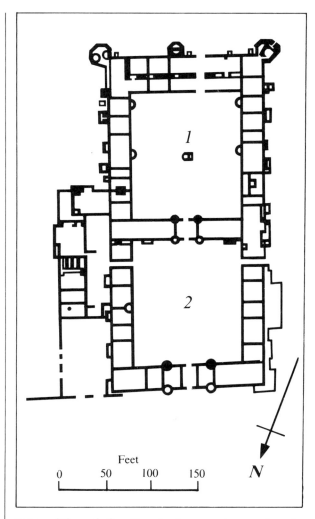

Palace of Nonsuch, Survey,
as excavated in 1959

1 *Inner Court*
2 *Outer Court*

hedges, topiary and various extravagant decorations. Of all this nothing survives save some fragments of the stucco and slate discovered by archaeological excavation in 1959. It was recorded in its heyday, however, by the artists Speed and Hofnaegel and by John Evelyn, the diarist, who described it in 1665 shortly before its acquisition and demolition by Charles II's grasping mistress, Barbara Villiers, Duchess of Cleveland:

I supped in Nonsuch House, whither the Office of Exchequer was transferred, and took an exact view of the plaster statues and bassrelievos inserted betwixt the timbers and puncheons of the outside walls of the court. I much admired how they had lasted so well and entire since the time of Henry VIII, exposed as they are to the air; and pity it is that they are not taken out and preserved in some dry place . . . The Palace consists of two courts, of which the first is of stone, castle-like, by the Lord Lumleys (of whom it was purchased), the other of timber, a Gothic fabric, but these walls incomparably beautified. I observed that the appearing timber puncheons entrelices, etc., were all so covered with scales of slate, that it seemed carved in the wood and painted, the slate fastened on the timber in pretty figures, that has, like a coat of armour, preserved it from rotting.

The death of Henry VIII in 1547 brought to an end the great age of Tudor palace building. His successors built hardly anything. Edward VI was too young and his reign too short, Mary's reign was short and blighted with tragedy, while

Elizabeth was too parsimonious. When Henry died the palaces of the King of England were more numerous and on a larger scale than those of any other king in Europe and the Italian Renaissance style had secured a firm foothold at court. The Reformation, the loss of the Crown's last continental possession, followed by the isolationist foreign policy of Elizabeth and her chief minister Lord Burghley, cut England off from the mainstream of European culture for half a century. While the Kings of France and Spain were embarking on the Louvre, the Tuilleries and the Escorial, nothing at all was built by the English Crown beyond small temporary structures and minor alterations – a timber Banqueting House at Whitehall and a Gallery at Windsor. On the other hand, Henry VIII's architectural extravagance had left his successors with more palaces than they could possibly need and some of them, including Bridewell, New Hall and Nonsuch, were alienated from the Crown by Edward VI and Mary. Elizabeth, however, still had as her principal houses Whitehall, St James's, Hampton Court, Greenwich, Eltham, Richmond, Windsor, Hatfield, Oatlands, Winchester and Woodstock, together with Somerset House (built by the Lord Protector Somerset during the minority of Edward VI and acquired by the Crown on the accession of Mary), and, following the death of Lord Lumley, she took back Nonsuch too. At the opening of her reign the Austrian ambassador had written to the Archduke Charles, a potential suitor:

I have seen several fine summer residences that belong to Queen Elizabeth, in two of which (Greenwich being one) I have been myself, and I may say that there are none in the world so richly garnished with costly furniture of silk, adorned with gold, pearls and precious stones. Then she has some twenty other houses, all of which might justly be called royal summer residences. Hence she is well worth the trouble.[17]

Elizabeth spent a varying time in all her principal residences and also went on her famous progresses in the summer, staying at the houses of her leading nobles at their expense. As William Harrison put it: 'When it pleaseth her in the summer season to recreate herself abroad, and view the estate of the country, every nobleman's house is her palace.'[18] She left London in June and stayed away till October, moving in a huge cavalcade of coaches and courtiers from house to house and taking with her three or four hundred carts laden with luggage and as many as 2,000 horsemen. Von Wedel described one of Elizabeth's returns to Whitehall.

Riding ahead were her servants, then followed two of her guard, then came her equerries and then her chamberlains, of whom there were about twenty. Then came the Privy Councillors. With them rode the Archbishop of Canterbury with 50 of his own horsemen. Elizabeth herself in a golden coach was preceded by Burghley and Walsingham. The Queen sitting all alone in her splendid coach appeared like a Goddess such as painters are want to depict. Behind her rode Leicester as Master of the Horse & more of the Privy Council, the 24 maids of honour followed by 50 more of the Queen's Guard.[19]

IV

THE ROYAL HOUSEHOLD FROM THE SIXTEENTH TO THE EIGHTEENTH CENTURIES

The royal household in the Middle Ages had occupied a central place in the government of England, and was the principal source of political authority. Its departments, especially the Chamber and the Wardrobe, rivalled the original agencies of national administration – the Exchequer and the Law – which had 'gone out of court' in the twelfth century. In the Middle Ages the institutions of government had depended for their vitality and force on the existence of an able and energetic King, with a zealous household, often formally duplicating the work of the out-of-court bureaucracy. When the King had been inadequate, as in the case of Henry VI, the government of the country had broken down.

The administrative reforms of Henry VIII and Thomas Cromwell in the first half of the sixteenth century permanently altered the character of the royal household and restricted its role in national life. They set up an independent bureaucracy responsible for the day-to-day machinery of government – the privy council, the Secretary, new revenue courts, and an elaborated exchequer.[1] All this reduced the importance of the household as an instrument of national administration and converted it into more of a purely domestic institution. From the sixteenth century onwards the royal household was increasingly separated from government administration and became merely the social setting of the monarch and the organization which catered for his personal needs. It was still a vast and important institution, far larger than the private household of even the greatest noble, and it retained a degree of political importance down to the nineteenth century with some blurring of staff between it and central government. A number of officials remained nominally in the household and were paid by the household treasurer, though their work made them part of the central bureaucracy. The 'messengers of the Chamber', for instance, were diplomatic couriers. The great officers of the household continued to be important men in politics well into the eighteenth century and access to the King was as essential for any member of his government as a seat in Parliament is today. Attendance at court was obligatory for any politically active peer or member or parliament. Occasional absence might be excused, but persistent absence could be construed as political opposition. The importance of attendance at court is demonstrated in the reign of Charles II by the way in which the extreme Protestants tried to destroy the political influence of the Catholic faction by forbidding popish recusants access to Whitehall Palace, thereby hoping to cut them off from the centre of power. But the institution of the household, as opposed to its personnel, played little part in national affairs after the sixteenth century.

The separation of government bureaucracy from the household did not immediately deprive the King's household of its social and political importance. It continued to be the focus of the struggle for power and patronage because those officers of the highest rank, whose duties gave them access to the royal presence, had more opportunity to play at politics behind the scenes than those who had the general entrée but were not frequently in the royal presence.[2]

The secession of the government administration from the household was only one aspect of Henry VIII's ordinances and reforms in the 1520s and 1530s. He also re-organized the household itself in order to make it function more effectively in its reduced role of supplying the daily necessities of the monarch's life and maintaining the appropriate ceremonial background to the court. The basic shape of the household was codified in the form in which it had developed in the later Middle Ages with three main departments: the Lord Chamberlain's department, the household below stairs, and the stables. The household below stairs was a vast catering department under the supervision of the Lord Steward. The stables looked after all the carriages and horses and came under the control of the Master of the Horse. The only later addition to this basic structure was the establishment of a separate bedchamber department by King James I in the early seventeenth century. This was staffed by the gentlemen and grooms of the bedchamber under the supervision of the Groom of the Stole and was essentially a body of personal servants responsible for the King's private apartments.

The Lord Chamberlain's department was the largest part of the household and combined the ancient departments of the chamber and the wardrobe. It centred on the public or state rooms above stairs and was responsible for most of the ceremonial and public side of court life, though at the grandest end of the scale there was some overlapping of responsibility with the Earl Marshal, one of the four Great Officers of State. In the Middle Ages the Earl Marshal had been responsible for the royal household in the field when the court still had some of the character of a battle horde. Gradually the Earl Marshal's department, with its staff of heralds, was restricted to supervising specific state occasions such as coronations or the funerals of monarchs, while the Lord Chamberlain gradually assumed responsibility for everything else. His staff included the ushers and grooms of the Presence and Privy Chambers and the Wardrobe staff, as well as the Master of the Musick, the chaplains and choir of the Chapel Royal. Each state room was staffed by its own separate officers and servants, and these people amounted to half the court above stairs. They were nearly all men. Women were employed in the royal household almost exclusively as domestic servants below stairs. As most of the staff continued to move round with the court, as in medieval households, the royal palaces had very small permanent staffs. The court proper was only constituted when the sovereign was in residence, and there was no large domestic organization permanently attached to any one palace. The bedchamber staff, the ushers and grooms of the state rooms, the kitchen, the stables and the other essential servants were all peripatetic. When the King was not in residence, the upkeep and cleaning of the palaces were entirely the responsibility of the Housekeeper and her own small permanent staff.

The household below stairs was the responsibility of the Lord Steward and the Board of the Green Cloth. There was a tendency as the centuries passed for many household positions to become sinecures and for extraordinary and inconvenient anomalies to develop. Thus by the late eighteenth century the

Hampton Court. The Wine Cellar.

business of getting a fire lit in the state rooms of an English royal palace was not very easy. Laying a fire in the grate was the responsibility of the Lord Steward because it appertained to the household below stairs, while actually lighting the fire was the responsibility of the Lord Chamberlain.

The Lord Steward with the assistance of the cofferers of the greencloth attempted to regulate the expenditure and the work of the household below stairs, which consisted of sixteen clearly defined sub-departments, each with its own head officer and separate staff of servants. They included the kitchen, the larder, the spicery, the acatry (for the preparation of meat), the poultry, the bakehouse, the wood-yard, the scullery, the pastry offices, the scalding house and the buttery. This organization of sub-offices was made permanent as a result of Henry VIII's reforms but had already begun to crystallize in the late fifteenth century. After 1660 it was partly superseded by a new, more economical system

Hampton Court. The
Great Kitchen.

of purveyance. Thereafter the royal household became much less self-supporting
and many of its provisions were received on contract from outside tradesman.
This enabled the number of the below stairs departments to be reduced. Meat,
for instance, ceased to be slaughtered on the premises. This had architectural
side-effects and resulted in the redundancy of a number of older office buildings.
The slaughterhouse at Whitehall, for example, was converted into a yard for the
sale of coal and wood in the later seventeenth century, and there was less need
for the royal palaces to be little self-supporting towns.[3]

The major architectural repercussion of developments in the household in the
reign of Henry VIII and later was not, however, on the domestic side, but above
stairs in the royal state rooms. The basic function of the court was to regulate
and formalize contact between the sovereign and his more important subjects.
Access to the King or Queen was the objective of every courtier, and the
essential problem in planning a royal palace was to arrange a succession of
rooms which would ensure an orderly progression for those with the privilege
of access – the entrée – and would also provide the monarch with private rooms
where he could retire. In early times, as has been noted, the only essential
rooms were the hall and chamber, but in the Middle Ages a more elaborate
sequence of rooms had developed, so that by the fifteenth century it was usual
for both the King and the Queen each to have their own separate apartments
and chapels. This duality of twin state apartments is one of the distinctive
features of English palace-planning down to the end of the eighteenth century
and it only finally ceased with George IV, who did not live with his wife.

The number of rooms in each apartment multiplied as their functions became
more specialized and more complex, a process which like many of the features
of the seventeenth and eighteenth-century household had begun under Henry
VIII. He was determined to secure more privacy and to devise a means of

Hampton Court. One of the Tudor rooms.

Hampton Court. Wolsey's Closet.

keeping away from courtiers who were trying to catch his eye or find him off guard in order to ask for some inconvenient favour or other. Henry even forbade the courtiers to follow him when he was hunting.[4] To avoid being besieged by the court he was forced to regulate the distance between himself and his courtiers by increasing the number of rooms and guarding their access more strictly. Where once there had just been the chamber, there was now the Guard Chamber, the Presence Chamber, the Privy Chamber and the Bed Chamber. Each of these rooms had a specific function. The Guard Chamber contained the Yeomen of the Guard (founded by Henry VII). Royal audiences were given in the Presence Chamber, and the Privy Chamber was a private room for the King to retire to, adjoining his bedchamber. The royal household ordinances promulgated by Henry VIII at Eltham in 1526 clearly defined access to these various rooms. 'Lords, knights, gentlemen, officers of the king's house and other honest personages' were allowed entrance to the Presence Chamber, but entrance to the Privy Chamber was more carefully restricted. 'Noe person, of what estate, degree or condicion soever he be, from henceforth presume, attempt or be in any wise suffered or admitted to come or repair into the king's privy chamber' except the servants on duty and persons invited by the King himself.[5] As for the bedchamber, no one was allowed to enter except the King's personal servants. The King himself only emerged from his private rooms for some specific purpose, such as going to the chapel or for some public ceremony or entertainment. He was careful to make these daily public ceremonies as magnificent as possible, a process which culminated in 'the astonishing epiphanies of Queen Elizabeth'.[6]

As the monarch retreated further from the Great Hall so the courtiers pressed further into the outer rooms, leading to an even longer enfilade in the King's apartment. The strict privacy of the Privy Chamber, as proclaimed by Henry VIII, was given up in the seventeenth century. In the reign of Charles I, the right of entry to the Queen's Privy Chamber was granted to the nobility, and it is probable that the King's too was open to courtiers in general. At the Restoration Sir Richard Leveson reported that the 'Court is modelling itself as it was in the late King's time, that is, that persons are to come near the King's person as they are in quality'. Charles II confirmed in his Household Regulations that persons waiting for business could enter the King's Privy Chamber.[7] Thus by the mid-seventeenth century the Privy Chamber was only slightly less public than the Presence Chamber. Its place as a private room between the public state apartment and the King's Bedchamber was taken by the 'Withdrawing Room'. Such a room was in existence as early as 1627 in the Queen's apartment at Whitehall and access to it was by personal invitation only, not by traditional right.[8] By the late seventeenth century the Withdrawing Room had undergone the same process of diminishing privacy as the Privy Chamber, and it in turn became the main room of assembly. When the Grand Duke of Tuscany, for instance, visited Whitehall in 1669, he was received by Charles II in the 'Withdrawing Room'.

Just as the royal household developed and split into specific subdivisions in the sixteenth and seventeenth centuries, so the state apartment divided into rooms designed to serve different aspects of the royal *persona*: rooms for state, public rooms for society, and the King's private rooms. One after the other the state rooms lost their original functions and became merely ante-rooms to the drawing room, which thus became the principal place for court assemblies. There the King most often met court society or received important foreigners.

7. PREVIOUS PAGE: *The Banqueting House, Whitehall. Ceiling by Rubens.*

8. ABOVE: *The Inner Gatehouse, Hampton Court.*

9. RIGHT: *The Queen's Chapel, St James's Palace.*

10. The Queen's House, Greenwich. Exterior.

11. Painted ceiling by Orazio Gentileschi from the hall of the Queen's House, Greenwich. Now at Marlborough House.

12. Wing of palace designed by John Webb at Greenwich.

13. St George's Hall, Windsor Castle. Watercolour from W. H. Pyne Royal Residences *(1819).*

Whitehall from St James's Park showing Charles II with his courtiers and spaniels.

Winchester Palace. An engraving showing Wren's layout with subsidiary buildings for the household and the Court.

Visitors approached by way of a courtyard, a grand staircase, and at the head of the stairs entered the Guard Chamber and then passed through the Presence and Privy Chambers into the drawing room, beyond which were the King's or Queen's private apartments. Each room retained its appropriate attendants – Yeomen of the Guard in the Guard Chamber, Gentlemen Ushers in the Presence Chamber, Gentlemen of the King's Chamber in the Privy Chamber, and the Groom of the Stole in the Drawing Room and the private rooms beyond – bedchamber, closet and so forth. Each of the principal reception rooms might still boast its canopy of state, marking the place where the King had once stood or sat, one, two or three hundred years before. Thus the history of the English court was encapsulated in the enfilade of the state apartment as it existed in the eighteenth century. The state apartments at Hampton Court which remain frozen as at the death of George II are the finest survival of their kind.[9]

Access to the more distant rooms in the long state enfilade continued to be graduated according to rank. This had been regulated once again by Charles II in his Household Ordinances and was re-confirmed by William III. In January 1685 Sir Charles Lyttelton wrote:

There is another thing which is now as much talked on: the new orders about the bedchamber . . . Nobody except the Duke (of York), Lord Ormond, and I think Hallifax, the two Secretaries of England and the Secretaries of Scotland are to come into the bedchamber without leave first asked; nor are they to ask leave if the King be in the

Hampton Court. The King's Guard Chamber, the first of the state apartments.

Windsor Castle. The
Queen's Privy Chamber.

closet. None under the degree of nobleman or privy councillor may ask leave at all,
unless he has business with the King.[10]

As they lost their original function the various state rooms became ante-rooms
for different grades of courtiers, until by the early nineteenth century the
modern arrangement had evolved, where a variable number of ante-rooms with
no specific function (just a guard room in a new-built palace like Buckingham
Palace but a series of fossilized state apartments in older palaces like St James's
and Windsor) led to the entrée room (the Green Drawing Room at Buckingham
Palace) for grandees, peers or accredited ambassadors to wait in, and then the
Throne Room itself where the monarch received. All these chambers made a
clearer separation possible between the public and private lives of the monarch.
George III and then Queen Victoria took the process to a logical conclusion by
building independent private houses for quiet family life in addition to the state
palaces used for the monarch's official business.

Throughout the seventeenth, eighteenth and into the nineteenth centuries
the English court was the chief focus of the nation's social life and its
perambulations determined the London Seasons. In the winter – approximately
from October or November to mid-May – the King was based at Whitehall, or
later at St James's. In the summer he moved to one or other of the country
palaces. The exact dates of his moves were determined by the weather and, in

Opposite above: St James's Palace. The Drawing Room, now the anteroom to the Throne Room.

Opposite below: St James's Palace. The Throne Room.

Buckingham Palace. The Green Drawing Room.

the eighteenth century, by the meeting of Parliament. Attendance at court was the essential qualification for being 'in' socially. This meant above all going to the royal drawing rooms (the event taking its name from the place of assembly). They were held several evenings a week in the eighteenth century, though they became less regular in the early nineteenth century, and were discontinued by Queen Victoria after the death of Prince Albert in 1861. Drawing rooms were stiff, formal and rather dull occasions on the whole, though it is recorded that one man was thrown out for being 'drunk and saucy' at St James's Palace in 1718.[11] The King usually stood or sat at one end of the room and spoke to those who were nearest to him, the company forming a respectful semi-circle round him. The qualification for attendance was not as clearly defined as at some of the more hide-bound continental courts, and a certain amount of leeway was left for healthy social-climbing. The need to wear fashionable (i.e. expensive) clothes seems to have been the chief deterrent to the unworthy. Quality and

Windsor Castle. A design
for the King's Bedroom by
Sir Jeffry Wyatville
showing the state bed by
Georges Jacob.

style of dress therefore decided who got in on general court days, but the
etiquette was stricter on court show days, such as the King's birthday and the
anniversaries of his coronation and accession to the throne. There were also
occasional court balls and morning levées (the latter for men only). Ministers
(including foreign emissaries), great nobles and the major gentry, formed the
core of those who usually attended court, though there were some more exotic
introductions like Omai, the 'gentle savage' whom Captain Cook brought back
from the Pacific Islands and who was an ornament at the court of George III for
a time.

Another important development in the seventeenth century was a substantial
decrease in the size of the royal household. This was caused mainly by rapidly
rising costs and the resulting pressure for retrenchment. In the course of the
century whole sub-offices were abolished as well as individual posts being left
unfilled. The departments of tents and of the beds, a chandlery, a boulting
house and a wafery all passed into oblivion. William III abolished several
medieval court offices including the Esquire of the Body and many ancient
sporting posts. Statistics help to tell the story. In Charles I's reign there were
forty-six posts in the Hall. By 1714 only five survived, and four of those were
abolished by George I. In the early seventeenth century there were two hundred
Yeomen of the Guard. In 1700 there were just one hundred. Under Charles I
there were ninety-seven grooms in the stables. Under George I there were only
seventy-two. In the course of the seventeenth century the household below
stairs decreased from 300 to 160 people. Altogether the royal household was
reduced from 1450 servants under Charles I to 950 under George I.[12] This
reduction in the size of the household meant that less accommodation was
needed for the permanent inhabitants of the court while at the same time more
space was needed for public rooms as the governing class and the social élite
(synonymous until the early twentieth century) increased in numbers.

V

THE STUART COURT

The reigns of James I and Charles I form one unified period in the history of the royal residences, sandwiched between the parsimony of Elizabeth and the watershed of the Civil War. The tragic finale colours our view of the achievement of the Stuart court, but in many ways it was a halcyon period of peace and enlightened patronage. Under the personally absurd but peace-loving James and the politically inept but cultivated Charles there was an officially sponsored flowering of the arts unequalled in post-medieval English history. This cultural achievement was the expression of a would-be absolute monarchy ruling by Divine Right. The palace projects, the art collections, the extravagant court masques all celebrated the power of the Crown and formed a 'symbolic justification of the royal policy'. In the King's palace at Whitehall and in the great London houses of the court aristocracy along the Thames were to be found some of the finest art collections ever assembled in England. In the various royal palaces fully-fledged Renaissance architecture was to be seen for the first time in England. Cultural and diplomatic ties between England and the continent were renewed for the first time since the Reformation and artistic contacts developed all over Europe from Spain to the Low Countries, from Copenhagen to Venice and even Rome. Architects, painters, sculptors and craftsmen were encouraged to come to London to embellish the royal palaces regardless of religious prejudice. The fragile fabric of this splendid court civilization was based on the peace which James I, and Charles I during the years of his personal government, sought to establish. This peace, the court culture and much of the Stuart architectural achievement were destroyed by the Civil War and the Interregnum. Its potential influence on the arts of England was largely discounted by the abrupt and destructive termination of the Stuart experiment at royal absolutism. Though the damage to Church and State was made good at the Restoration, the damage to the more delicate plant of the arts took longer to heal.

The key-figure in the creation of the settings of the court under James I and Charles I was, of course, Inigo Jones, the first and one of the greatest English classical architects. He entered the orbit of court patronage *circa* 1605 in the service of Queen Anne of Denmark, the consort of James I. In 1610 he was appointed surveyor to Henry, Prince of Wales and may have been involved in some internal alterations to St James's Palace where the Prince was establishing a library and picture gallery (the nucleus of the future royal collections), but this was cut short by the Prince's premature death in 1612. The following year Jones was granted the reversal of the post of Surveyor of the King's Works and succeeded on Simon Basil's death in 1615. From then till 1643 he was constantly engaged on a series of works at the various royal palaces. He was the autocrat of the works, an artistic reflection of the political absolutism of his masters. All the more important designs emanating from the Office of Works in his time bear the impress of his mind. The group of royal buildings erected by James I during Inigo Jones's surveyorship were of seminal importance in the history of English architecture and formed the inspiration for the spread of neo-Palladianism in the following century. The chief of them – the Banqueting House at Whitehall, the Queen's House at Greenwich, and the Queen's Chapel at St James's – fortunately still survive. They show Jones 'not only as a careful student of Palladio and Scamozzi but also as a mature architectural designer whose skill in composition was controlled by an intellectual grasp of the principles of Renaissance architecture. Nothing like these buildings had previously been seen in England, and in baroque Europe they were an unexpected reaffirmation of High Renaissance principle which found no contemporary parallel in France or Italy.'[1] The influence of Venetian Renaissance architecture on England was a direct result of basic political and economic similarities between the two countries, similarities which made Venice far more sympathetic to the English than the Papal or Spanish satellite governments in the other countries of the Italian peninsular. Though England was Protestant and a monarchy while Venice was technically Catholic and a republic, both countries were mercantile economies with similar aristocracies and had had close diplomatic and trading relations for over a hundred years. This made Venetian architecture both more sympathetic and more accessible to Englishmen than the baroque of Papal Rome.

Much of the architectural output of the Stuart court was of a transient nature. Settings for masques, triumphal arches, or funerary catafalques of timber, calico and plaster were as carefully designed, and formed as important a part of the *mis en scène* of the court, as solid buildings of brick and stone. It was in the court masque that Inigo Jones first displayed his skill as an Italian-trained designer. Between 1605 and 1640 he was responsible for staging over fifty masques and similar entertainments, often in collaboration with Ben Jonson. Over 450 drawings for costumes and settings for court masques by Jones survive. The first masque to be staged at Whitehall was the *Masque of Blackness*, a neo-Platonic allegory about the power of monarchy in 1605. It had sensational effects devised by Jones including an artificial sea with beasts and mermaids. *Hymenaei* the following year was staged to celebrate the wedding of Lady Frances Howard to the Earl of Essex. It began with a Roman wedding scene and there was a gigantic globe of gold and silver floating in mid-air. The *Masque of Queens* in 1609 was the most spectacular of the early masques and opened with a hell scene complete with fire and smoke which passed to reveal 'a glorious and magnificent building figuring the House of Fame . . . filled with several-coloured lights like emeralds, rubies, saphires, carbucles etc.'. The masques were more than great theatrical spectacles. Though professional actors played the speaking parts in the first half of the masques, representing disorder etc., the courtiers and royal family usually danced in the second half showing the triumph of Good and monarchical government. The masques were in fact idealized allegories of political power and promulgated theories about the monarchy, the divine nature of kingship, the obligations and perquisites of the Crown. They were not simply court balls or mere dressing up. Immense effort went into their detailed design and production. The results were the most sophisticated court spectacles which England had ever seen, though they were a development of the court revelries of the Tudors. Their precursors were the chivalric show-pieces staged by the Queen's Knights on Elizabeth's Accession Days, or the fêtes on her summer progresses with their romantic and classical mythology usually performed alfresco. But under the Stuarts these court spectacles became much more polished and elaborate.[2]

The settings of the masques related to other symbolic but temporary structures erected by the Stuarts, such as the triumphal arches put up for James I's coronation entry into London in March 1604. This was the first major state entry into London since 1559 and, though delayed for a year because of plague, was an event of unprecedented splendour. The timber triumphal arches erected for the occasion were designed by Stephen Harrison under the direction of Ben Jonson and Thomas Dekker. They displayed the accurate Renaissance scholarship which was to be the most notable feature of all the royal architectural work in the new reign. They represented the earliest acknowledged application of principles of harmonic proportion to architecture in England. Each arch was based on a series of ratios which, we are assured, depended on the 'Pythagoran-Platonic division of the Musical scale'. They were directly influenced by the arches erected at Antwerp for the entry of the Archduke Albert and Infanta Isabella in 1599, and their elaborate decoration with much strapwork and fantastic obelisks was more Netherlandish than Italianate.[3]

Some of the gardening done at the royal palaces in the early seventeenth century partook of a similarly theatrical character with *trompe-l'oeil* decoration on walls, and curious grottoes, fountains and follies. Perhaps the most elaborate was that laid out at Richmond on an extensive scale by Henry, Prince of Wales, and of which no trace now remains. It was designed with the help of two foreign architects, a Frenchman, Salomon de Caus, and an Italian, Constantino dei Servi. De Caus was sent over to England by the French ambassador in 1611 to design the waterworks at Richmond, though he had already been in England in 1607–8 when he did some garden work for Queen Anne of Denmark. In 1613 he went to Heidelberg to lay out a garden for Elizabeth, the eldest daughter of James I, and her husband Frederick V, Count Palatine of the Rhine. His nephew Isaac, however, stayed on in the service of the English court. Constantino dei Servi came from Florence and had previously worked for the Medici. He made designs for 'fountains, summer-houses, galleries and other things' at Richmond and Prince Henry paid him a salary of £200 a year. Nothing is known of the appearance of Prince Henry's extravaganza at Richmond, but it was recorded as having among other ornaments a 'great figure . . . three times as large as the one at Pratalino, with rooms inside, a dovecot in the head and grottoes in the base'.[4] The premature death of the Prince in November 1612 put an end to the scheme and removed an important royal patron of the arts.

The first substantial new royal building, as opposed to masque settings and gardens, in the reign of James I was the Queen's House at Greenwich. In the early part of the reign James had frequently used Greenwich Palace in the summer and had carried out some minor alterations there including walling the park and making a vaulted basement under the Great Hall. In 1613 he gave Greenwich to the Queen for her own use, it is said in order to secure her presence at the wedding of the King's favourite, Robert Carr, Earl of Somerset, to Frances Howard, Countess of Essex (who had divorced her first husband on

The Queen's House, Greenwich. The entrance front facing the river.

Oatlands. Design for a new chimneypiece in the Queen's apartments by Inigo Jones.

grounds of impotence). The Queen decided to build a new house, or trianon, on a site straddling the public road to Deptford from Woolwich and thus giving access from the palace gardens to the park on the other side of the road. This curious choice of site may not have been as original as it seems, however, for there was already an existing small Tudor gatehouse across the road in the same place. At least Anthony van Wyngaerde's drawing of Greenwich in the mid-sixteenth century shows a little gabled building where the Queen's House now stands.[5] The architect of the new house was Inigo Jones, whose first important architectural commission it was. His design was for a pair of oblong buildings, one in the palace garden and one in the park, joined together by a covered bridge over the road to form an H plan. Work progressed slowly and when the Queen died in 1619 ceased for ten years. It was only in 1629 that the house was given to another Queen, Henrietta Maria, wife of Charles I, and work continued into the 1630s.[6] As well as the new house at Greenwich, Queen Anne of Denmark also employed Jones at her other country palace, Oatlands in Surrey. There he designed a 'great gate to ye vineyard' and some interior alteration for the visit of the Venetian ambassador, Pietro Contarini, whom the Queen entertained to a banquet at Oatlands in 1617. Jones's last design for the Queen was the catafalque for her funeral in Westminster Abbey in 1619. It was considered 'the fairest and stateliest that I think was ever seen there'.[7]

James I himself undertook various improvements at Whitehall. In 1606 a new Banqueting House was built as a setting for the court masques to replace the timber one built for Elizabeth I in 1581. James's new one was 120 feet long by 53 feet wide and was built of stone with galleries of Ionic columns over Doric. It was inspired by a Roman basilica but its exact appearance and its architect are not known, though it was obviously expressive of advanced ideas. In January 1619 it was accidentally burnt to the ground by two workmen who, while cleaning, set fire with their candles to some oily rags and 'not able to quench, and fearing to be known that they did it, shut the doors, parting away without speaking thereof, till at last perceived by others, when it was too late and

Oatlands. Design by Inigo Jones for a gateway to the vineyard.

irrecoverable'. A new Banqueting House was immediately put in hand under the supervision of Inigo Jones. It was completed in 1622 and is a double cube of 110 feet by 55 feet, perfectly classical in style. 'Here for the first time in London was a building of Mediterranean monumentality establishing a new code of order and proportion.'[8] It became the touchstone for all future architectural developments at the palace. There was to be a series of proposals for rebuilding the rest to the same scale, but these all came to nothing and the Banqueting House remained a 'lonely fragment of intended grandeur'. The Banqueting House design was a direct outcome of Jones's close study of Palladio's and Scamozzi's work at Vicenza and Venice, undertaken in the company of the Earl of Arundel when they had both gone on to Italy after accompanying Princess Elizabeth and the Count Palatine to Heidelberg in 1612. It is not, however, a copy of any single building by Palladio but a new composition inspired by his work. Many of the individual elements – the alternating pediments over the windows, or the carved swags and masks in the frieze – are derived from Palladio's palaces, but they are combined in a new way. As first built the elevations were a subtle exercise in polychrome masonry, the plinth being of pale yellow Oxfordshire stone, the walls of brown Northamptonshire stone and only the balustrade and the details of Portland stone. The interior is one large room over a vaulted basement where in 1623 Isaac de Caus made a rustic grotto

The Queen's House, Greenwich, Principal Floor

1 *Upper Part of Hall*
2 *Staircase*
3 *Queen's Drawing Room*
4 *Queen's Bedroom*
5 *Loggia*

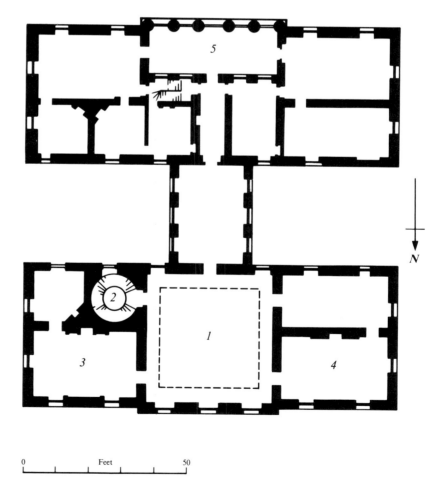

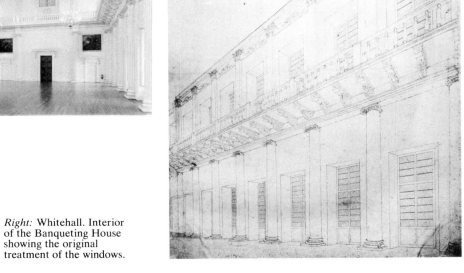

Top: Whitehall. The Banqueting House.

Above: Whitehall. Interior of the Banqueting House.

Right: Whitehall. Interior of the Banqueting House showing the original treatment of the windows.

to which more 'shell-worke' was added in 1625 but has since all disappeared.[9] The hall itself survives largely in its original form, though an apsidal niche at one end was removed soon after completion. It is a plain rectangle with a balustraded balcony round the middle of the walls, two tiers of pilasters reflecting the external treatment and a noble ceiling with large oval and rectangular panels at first left plain. At the same time as the rebuilding of the Banqueting House James I also erected, in 1619–20, new lodgings for George Villiers, Marquess (later Duke) of Buckingham, who had succeeded Somerset as the King's favourite. They were 'towards the privie garden' but the exact location is uncertain. Some of Inigo Jones's designs for elaborate ceilings with the Villiers arms survive.[10]

James I's preferred summer residence was not one of the numerous existing royal palaces but Theobalds in Hertfordshire, a former private house which he acquired from Robert Cecil, Earl of Salisbury, following a visit in 1607. James was so impressed by Theobalds that he asked for it and suggested offering to Cecil in exchange the gloomy old palace of Hatfield (a fifteenth-century brick quadrangle which had come to the Crown from the Bishop of Ely at the dissolution of the monasteries and where both Mary and Elizabeth had spent some time). Hatfield was old-fashioned. Theobalds, however, had been rebuilt by Robert Cecil's father Lord Burghley in the 1570s and was one of the largest and grandest houses in England. It was built of stone round two regular courtyards with the hall in the dividing range. The inner court, called the Fountain Court, was 84 feet square with towers in the corners. James spent much time at Theobalds, hunting in the park, which he enlarged in 1620 and enclosed with a brick wall nine and a half miles round; fragments of this still stand. In 1625 Inigo Jones designed a new Banqueting House for Theobalds but this may not have been executed, for James I died on 21 March of that year, and was succeeded by his surviving son, Charles, the greatest art-collector in the history of the English royal family.

Charles I's reputation as a 'Maecenas of the arts' has disguised the fact that his architectural activity was strictly curtailed by the straitened circumstances of the Exchequer. In the early part of the reign he built little for himself. Most of the work in the royal residences was done for Queen Henrietta Maria, rather than for the King. The two major new works associated with Charles I, the Newmarket Lodge and the Queen's Chapel at St James's, were in fact executed

Left: Newmarket Lodge. Inigo Jones's first design.

Right: Newmarket Lodge. Inigo Jones's second design.

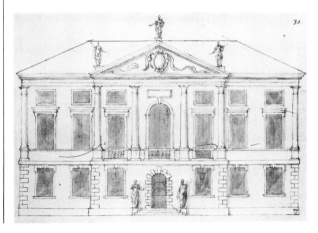

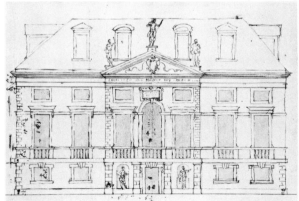

and paid for in the previous reign when the Crown finances were not as tight as they became under Charles. The Lodge at Newmarket was put in hand in 1619. Two designs by Inigo Jones survive, each for a seven bay two-storeyed house with a hipped roof and dormer windows. The more ambitious preliminary scheme shows a pedimented frontispiece with columns, while the other is astylar and simpler. This important little building had a very short life and was demolished in 1650 without any adequate record being made of its appearance. The building accounts suggest that it was a version of the astylar design but only five bays wide. It may have had a double cube hall, and the outbuildings included a Tuscan brewhouse.[11] The Newmarket Lodge was one of a series of small lodges designed for Charles by Inigo Jones, including one built at Bagshot near Windsor with a timber portico in 1631–3 and one in Hyde Park of two storeys, with stuccoed brick elevations, a loggia of Composite columns, and six dormers in the roof, built in 1634–5.[12] Though shortlived, these little houses were important in the history of English architecture because the drawings for them were used in the eighteenth century as a model for the Georgian neo-Palladian villa.

The other important work begun for Charles while he was Prince of Wales was the new chapel on the east side of St James's Palace, which miraculously still stands. It was begun as a consequence of the proposed marriage of Charles to the Infanta of Spain which made necessary a Catholic chapel. The foundation stone was laid on 16 May 1623. In the event the Spanish marriage fell through, and the interior was fitted up in 1625 for a French-born Queen, Henrietta Maria. The pedimented west front with lugged architraves to the windows is similar to the astylar design for Newmarket. The interior is an exquisite example of Inigo Jones's classical style, incorporating a 'Venetian' window derived from Scamozzi over the altar. This is the earliest example of this popular device in English architecture and set a fashion which has lasted into the twentieth century. The magnificent coffered segmental ceiling is based on Palladio's hypothetical restoration of the vault of the Temple of Venus at Rome. The Queen's Closet at first-floor level at the west end was originally separated from the church by a screen of Corinthian pilasters. This screen has gone, but the chimneypiece in the closet, made of Reigate stone, survives in the form shown in Jones's drawing for it.[13]

The Queen's House at Greenwich, like the St James's chapel originally begun for somebody else, was also completed by Charles I for Henrietta Maria, between 1629 and 1635. The interior decoration was richer and more French, to suit the Queen's taste, than Jones's earlier Italianate work for the court. One of the chimneypiece designs, for instance, is endorsed in Jones's hand 'from the French ambaseter', which suggests that he was supplied with drawings by French architects to guide him.[14] In any case Jones had visited Paris in 1609 so had first-hand knowledge of up-to-date French architecture. On the other hand much of the craftsmanship was English. The marble floor of the hall and the woodcarving of the ceilings and the hall balustrade was executed under the direction of Nicholas Stone, the King's Master Mason. Much of the painted decoration, however, was executed by continental artists of the first rank. The hall ceiling was painted by Orazio Gentileschi (a Tuscan artist who came to England in 1626 at the invitation of the Duke of Buckingham) with Apollo and the Muses (now removed to Marlborough House), while the Queen's Drawing Room was enriched with paintings by Jordaens (now lost), and Rubens too was consulted. The only paintings to survive *in situ* are the colourful arabesques, or

St James's. The Queen's Chapel begun in 1623.

Below: St James's. The Queen's Chapel. Inigo Jones's design for the chimneypiece in the royal pew.

Above: The Queen's House. Design for a fountain by Inigo Jones.

grotteschi, on the coving of the Queen's Bedroom, possibly by John de Critz I (the Sergeant Painter to the King) or by Matthew Gooderick. Their antique Roman style can only be matched today by the contemporary ceiling in the Single Cube Room at Wilton. Though stripped of its rich fittings during the Civil War, much of the basic architecture of the Queen's House survives. The hall is a single cube of forty feet and retains some of its original colouring and the gilding of the gallery balustrade and ceiling beams. The design of the ceiling with a central circular panel surrounded by rectangular ones with circles in the corners is similar to that in the Banqueting House. The balustraded gallery has no Italian precedent and is an innovation on Jones's part to provide communication between the principal first-floor rooms. The circular staircase which gives

Right: The Queen's House. A design for a chimney-piece by Inigo Jones.

Far right: The Queen's House. The hall. The ceiling originally contained paintings by Orazio Gentileschi now at Marlborough House.

Below: The Queen's House. The staircase.

Opposite: The Queen's House. Ceiling of the Queen's Bedroom, the cove painted with colourful arabesques probably by John de Critz I, Sergeant Painter to the King.

access to these forms a graceful spiral of white marble steps and has a pretty wrought-iron balustrade. It is one of Inigo Jones's most beautiful creations.

Of Jones's other work for Queen Henrietta Maria nothing now survives. The suite of rooms at Wilton (even if they are by John Webb rather than Inigo Jones) are a unique reminder of the vanished court style of Charles I and Henrietta Maria. They are the only visual clues to the appearance of the lost rooms at Whitehall, Somerset House, Oatlands and Wimbledon. Somerset House was given to the Queen on her marriage in 1625 and work there was continuous from 1626 to 1637. The Queen was also given Oatlands, and Jones designed new chimneypieces and ceilings there as well as garden decorations,[15] while at least one of the ceiling paintings was by Simon Vouet, the distinguished contemporary French artist. In 1639 Charles bought Wimbledon, another house of the Cecils, for the Queen, and it became her favourite country residence. The gardens were laid out anew for her by a Frenchman, André Mollet, and some of the interior was done up by Inigo Jones.

Somerset House, the quadrangular Tudor palace of the Protector Somerset in the Strand, became the town palace of the Queens of England in 1617 when James I gave it to Anne of Denmark. Henrietta Maria made substantial alterations under the direction of Inigo Jones. A Cabinet Room was built in 1626 at the end of the Privy Gallery, with an iron balcony aligned on the axis of the watergate. This Cabinet Room should not be confused with the New Cabinet Room formed in 1628 out of an older room at the east end of the Cross Gallery. It too was given an iron balcony with a view over the river. The building accounts convey the impression of a richly marbled, coloured, and gilded ensemble. The decoration was white, gold and blue, ornamented with grotesque work. But only a drawing of an elegant doorway survives to give a clearer idea of what it was like. Both Cabinet Rooms were used for the display of the Queen's pictures.

In 1630–5 a cruciform Catholic chapel was built at the east end of the palace on the site of the old tennis court. This formed a double cube of 60 by 30 feet with shallow transepts, a vestry behind the altar, and a royal closet at the other end. It was sumptuously decorated and was one of Jones's most important interiors. The altarpiece was painted by Rubens. Though badly damaged in the Civil War, the chapel was repaired afterwards and survived till the mid-eighteenth century when it was demolished to make way for the new Somerset House by Sir William Chambers. The royal closet or pew was painted by John de Critz: the ceiling with grotesque work on a white ground and the walls grained to represent walnut with gilding and panels of grotesque work.[16] It was separated from the body of the chapel by an elegant two-tier screen in the French style. The completion of the chapel was followed by the reconstruction of the interior of the Cross Gallery. Finally Jones provided a design for replacing the old Strand front with a grand new classical facade 480 feet long. This was not executed, but Henrietta Maria did get the chance to rebuild the centre of the river front following her return to Somerset House at the Restoration in 1660. At that time John Webb added the Jonesian frontispiece with an arcaded ground floor and Corinthian pilasters above.

At Whitehall in the 1630s Jones continued to design the series of splendid masques. Such spectacles formed an essential part of the way Charles I saw himself and wished others to see their monarch too. The theatre was very much part of the King's natural habitat. 'No other English monarch was so intensely concerned with his own image, and in the splendid series of masques that Jones created for him in the 1630s, we may see the royal imagination fashion through the art of his Master Surveyor as with Van Dyck and Rubens an ideal realm and an ideal self.'[17] Charles had Henry VIII's cockpit reconstructed as a theatre by Jones in 1629–31. The interior kept its old octagonal form but was given a semi-circular stage, possibly based on the original treatment of Palladio's Teatro Olimpico at Vicenza before the deep perspectives were added by Scamozzi. The Cockpit-in-Court theatre was chiefly used for masques, but it could also be transformed if necessary to a simple illusionistic theatre. In 1637, the year in which Charles told his nephew that he was the happiest monarch in Christendom, Jones designed for him a special new Masquing Room at Whitehall as an alternative to the Banqueting House. This was made necessary by the installation of Rubens's great ceiling paintings in 1635. Charles was afraid that they might be damaged by the smoke from the torches used during the masques.

The Banqueting House ceiling was the crowning glory of Stuart patronage and is the only one of Rubens's larger baroque schemes to remain in the

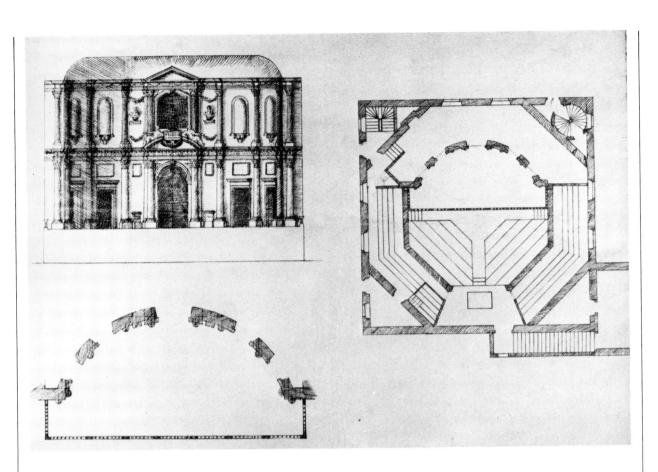

Whitehall. Inigo Jones's design for the Cockpit Theatre which was constructed within Henry VIII's shell, 1629–31.

architectural setting for which it was intended. The ceiling panels were commissioned by Charles I while Rubens was in England in 1629 and 1630. They were painted in Antwerp and completed in 1634. They cost £3,000, in addition to which the grateful King gave Rubens a gold chain and a baronetcy. The subject of the ceiling is the apotheosis of James I, with Justice, Zeal, Religion, Honour and Victory. On the south panel the King points to Peace and Plenty. On his left Minerva is driving Rebellion to Hell. The north panel alludes to the Union of the English and Scottish crowns. The corner panels represent Bounty trampling on Avarice, Government trampling on Rebellion, Hercules clubbing Envy, and Minerva spearing Lust. The overall concept is a glorification of a king by Divine Right.

Charles I's chief personal contribution to Whitehall was in the form of works of art rather than large-scale new architecture. Many of the paintings commissioned or collected by him were, however, intended for particular positions. The large equestrian portrait of the King, for example, by Van Dyck was intended for the end of the Long Gallery, where it looked to the observer as if the King was about to ride into the room through a triumphal arch. Much of Charles I's patronage of contemporary artists such as Gentileschi, Rubens, Honthorst and Jordaens was in order to obtain decorative paintings to be incorporated into particular architectural ensembles. He already had an important collection of masterpieces when he ascended the throne, having inherited the pictures of his mother and brother in addition to many gifts from foreign heads of state. He continued to add throughout his reign, especially the works of Venetian masters.

Whitehall. The ground plan of Inigo Jones's proposed new palace for Charles I, 1638.

His greatest triumph, diplomatic as well as cultural, was his acquisition of the fabulous Gonzaga collection from Mantua. John de Critz, the Sergeant-Painter, was paid in March 1639 for repairing the Mantua pictures on their arrival in England. These collections transformed Whitehall into an amazing museum of art. Rubens on his visit to England in 1629 wrote 'when it comes to fine pictures by the hands of first-rate masters, I have never seen such a large number in one place as in the royal palace.' Some of the finest small pictures were kept in a special cabinet room designed by Abraham Vanderdoort, the Keeper of the King's Pictures, but the larger paintings and sculptures were distributed throughout the palace. The Long Gallery contained 102 paintings, with statues in front of the windows silhouetted against the light.[18]

In the last years of the reign the King seriously contemplated rebuilding Whitehall as a large symmetrical classical complex twice as large as the Escorial, grouped round a series of monumental courtyards, into one of which the Banqueting House was to be incorporated. The earliest mention of this proposed new palace was in 1638, when it was rumoured that 'His Majesty hath a desire to build new again in a more uniform sort'. This palace, if executed, would have been Inigo Jones's greatest work, but it was frustrated by Charles I's accumulating financial and political difficulties, and was never even begun. Today it is represented by a large and confusing series of drawings in the hand of Jones's pupil and associate, John Webb.[19] They fall into two groups comprising seven separate schemes. Only one of these can be confidently attributed to Jones himself, and even this is known only from drawings by Webb. It was, however, the starting point for all the abortive schemes for a new Whitehall which stretch from the reign of Charles I to William III, and so has an architectural significance which 'transcends its ephemeral character as the . . . dream of a powerless monarch'.[20]

Charles I's new Whitehall is the greatest 'might-have-been' in the history of English architecture. It would have been a palace over 1,000 feet long and nearly 1,000 feet deep, covering a site of twenty-three acres. If executed, it would have exceeded in size and grandeur the only comparable palaces of the time: the (incomplete) Louvre-Tuileries and the Escorial. The sources for Jones's design, however, were not those 'modern' buildings, but classical antiquity as reconstructed in Palladian source books – Palladio's 1584 edition of Vitruvius or Scamozzi's reconstruction of Pliny's villa at Laurentium with its great circular atrium, surely the inspiration for the circular courtyard in the Whitehall designs. Scamozzi was the major source – arguably a more important influence on Jones's architecture than Palladio himself – and the central block on the river front was based on a design, in Jones's possession, by Scamozzi for a Venetian municipal palace. Various Italian, French and antique sources are synthesized in the Whitehall designs into an harmonious and understated whole – serene and grand. The visual impact of this huge palace with its calm basilican interiors – Great Hall, Council Chamber and Chapel – would have been that of a palace in ancient Rome, perhaps the Palatine itself. But it was not to be. In March 1639 the King left Whitehall, unimproved, to take up arms against the Scots, an event which marked the opening of the English Civil War. In January 1642, following his unsuccessful attempt to arrest five members of the House of Commons, he left Whitehall and did not return till his trial and execution. The palace, where in Charles's reign meals had been served at eighty-six tables every day, was deserted. A graphic description of the empty palace was printed in the same year:

To begin at the entrance into the Court, where there had wont to be a continuall throng, either of Gallants standing to ravish themselves with the sight of Ladies hansome legs and Insteps as they tooke Coach; Or of the tribe of guarded Liveries, by whom you could scarce passe without a jeare or a saucy answer to your question; now if you would ask a question there is no body to make answer . . .

You may without a rub, walke into the Hall, for surely there are no strong smells out of the Kitching to delight your Nostrells withall, no Provision to bee sould, nor the greasie Scullions to bee seene over Head and Eares in a Kettle full of Kidnies, nor anything else to stoppe your progresse into the House . . .

If you steppe up Staires to the Guard Chamber, where His Majesties great Beefe-eaters had wont to sit in attendance on their places, which was nothing but to tell Tales, devoure the beaverage, keepe a great fire, carry up Dishes . . . now they are all vanisht, nothing left but the bare Walls, and a cold Harth, from whence the Fire-irones are removed too, and as its thought converted into shoes for light Horses. The great black-Jackes set under the Table, all full of Cobwebs . . .

You may walke into the Presence Chamber with your Hat, Spurres and sword on, And if you will presume to be so unmannerly, you may sit downe in the Chaire of State . . .

If you be minded to survey the Lodgings and withdrawing rooms, you shall finde those rich and costly hangings of Persian Arras and Turkey worke (like the Bishops) for their pride taken downe . . .

In the Cockpit and Revelling Roomes, where at a Play or Masque the darkest night was converted to the brightest Day that ever shin'd, by the luster of Torches, the sparkling of rich Jewells . . . now you may goe in without a Ticket or the danger of a broken pate, you may enter at the Kings side, walke rounde about the Theaters, view the Pullies, the Engines . . . but all in a dumbe silence, as the Pallace stood not neere a well peopled City but as if it were the decay'd buildings of ruin'd Troy.[21]

In 1643 in anticipation of an attack on London by the royalist forces, Parliament fortified the City and erected a battery between the Banqueting House and the 'Holbein Gate' so devised as to sweep the approaches to the palace from Charing Cross. In the following year steps were taken to purge Whitehall of all Papists and wives or children or servants of people 'in service against Parliament'. A certain amount of organized iconoclasm was also set in motion. The stained glass in the Chapel Royal was smashed and replaced with clear glazing, the organs removed, and the paintings of religious subjects on panels were planed off. Parliamentary troops were quartered in the palace in 1648. The final tragedy took place there the following year. The King was brought back to London for his trial by Parliament and lodged either at Whitehall 'in his usual Bed-Chamber' or at St James's. His execution took place at Whitehall on 30 January. On the morning he was brought from St James's across the park, up the stairs to the Tiltyard Gallery over the 'Holbein Gate', into the Green Chamber. After resting he was led out through the Banqueting House to the scaffold, which had been erected in front of that building, and there beheaded. Following the death of the King, Parliament set about dispersing the furnishings of the palace and the King's art collection. Only the Mantegna 'Triumphs' and the Raphael 'Cartoons' were retained. But the fabric of the palace was saved when in 1654 the Lord Protector Cromwell took it over as his official residence and preserved much of the remaining furnishing for his own use. When Evelyn visited Whitehall in February 1656, he 'found it very glorious and well-furnished, as far as I could safely go, and was glad to find they had not much defaced that rare piece of Henry VII etc. (by Holbein) done on the walls of the King's Privy Chamber.'[22] The other palaces fared worse. Somerset House was sacked and the chapel in particular greatly damaged. At Greenwich the Queen's House was stripped of its fine fittings and the Tudor palace despoiled and used as a jail for Dutch prisoners. Newmarket, Oatlands, Richmond and Theobalds were totally destroyed. What Henry VIII and Thomas Cromwell had done to the monasteries and medieval shrines, Parliament and Oliver Cromwell did to the royal palaces of England.

VI

THE RESTORATION

The Civil War marked a turning point in the history of the English royal residences. It was the cause, immediate or indirect, of the destruction of most of those medieval or Tudor palaces which had made the King of England one of the best housed monarchs in Europe. Greenwich, Newmarket, Nonsuch, Oatlands, Richmond, Theobalds, Winchester and Woodstock were all demolished during the Civil War or shortly afterwards. The gap caused by such an architectural holocaust was never made good, though this was not for want of trying on the part of late seventeenth-century monarchs and their architects. Charles II came back to the throne in 1660 with the serious intention of rebuilding all his palaces on a scale of continental baroque grandeur as a demonstration of the vitality of the restored monarchy. A worthy start was made on new palaces at Greenwich and Winchester; Windsor was sweepingly remodelled, Holyrood house rebuilt, and much piecemeal work was done at Whitehall, though nothing came of Webb and Wren's proposals for a complete rebuilding there. The trouble was that Charles II's finances were not equal to his ambitions and no later monarch was able to continue his momentum. Nearly everything he inaugurated was left unfinished. Only the shell of one wing of Greenwich was built before work was abandoned. Winchester was left an incomplete shell at the time of his death and was later turned into barracks. Holyrood and Windsor were hardly ever lived in by his immediate successors. When Whitehall was destroyed by fire in 1698, the heaven-sent opportunity for at last carrying out Wren's plans for an English Louvre or Escorial were passed by, and instead the site was redeveloped as a street of private houses and government offices. For want of anything better the dreary little Tudor palace of St James's became in the eighteenth century the sole metropolitan palace of the Kings of England.

In 1660 Charles II was determined to re-establish the monarchy in all its old glory. To this end he commissioned splendid baroque crown jewels and rich chapel plate to replace the treasures melted down under the Commonwealth, and he set about reconstituting the English royal residences on the strength of a revenue grant of £1,200,000 a year from Parliament.[1] This income, however, was not a set sum like the modern civil list. It consisted of the grant of specific revenues, chiefly the Customs and Excise, which it was hoped would bring in the necessary amount of money. But in fact it varied from year to year and fell substantially short of the desired sum. This left the King less well-off than

St James's. The plate for the Chapel Royal commissioned by Charles II at the Restoration in 1660.

intended and caused a royal financial crisis in 1672, which in turn curtailed many of the King's more ambitious palace-building projects.

Charles II's first act on his return was to recover as much as possible of the dispersed contents of the royal palaces. In June 1660 Evelyn recorded that plate, hangings, pictures and so forth were then daily being brought in. Seventeen cartloads of stuff were recovered from Cromwell's widow alone. The state rooms at Whitehall were not in too bad condition, having been occupied by Cromwell as Lord Protector of England, but Charles had them re-painted and gilded, marble paving laid down, and general works of refurbishment carried out under the direction of John Webb. One of the first rooms to be done up was Charles I's 'Cabinet Room', where some of the smaller items in the royal collection were displayed. Evelyn visited it on 1 November 1660.

I went with some of my relations to Court to show them his Majesty's cabinet and closet of rarities; the rare miniatures of Peter Oliver, after Raphael, Titian and other masters, which I infinitely esteem; also that large piece of the Duchess of Lennox, done in enamel by Pettitot, and a vast number of agates, onyxes and intaglios, especially a medallion of Caesar, as broad as my hand; likewise rare cabinets of pietracommessa . . .[2]

These preliminary works, however, were aimed merely at making Whitehall habitable in the short term and Charles contemplated making a clean sweep of the whole palace (except for the Banqueting House) and starting again from scratch, as his father had intended on the eve of the Civil War. For though parts of the existing fabric were magnificent, especially some of the interiors, it had no overall architectural form and the twenty-five acre complex with its 2,000 rooms looked more like a little town than one building. Count Magalotti, who accompanied the Grand Duke of Tuscany to England in 1669, described it as 'more remarkable for its situation than for the nobleness of its structure, being nothing more than an assemblage of several houses, badly built at different times and for different purposes' – it had 'nothing in it from which you could suppose it to be the habitation of the King'.[3] In autumn 1661 John Webb submitted plans, based on those of Inigo Jones, for a huge new Classical complex, ordered round half a dozen courtyards and taking the cue for its detailing from the Banqueting House.[4] For practical and financial reasons nothing came of these proposals. A serious deterrent to any large-scale architectural project at Whitehall was the impossibility of evicting the colonies of courtiers from their official lodgings.

Instead the King contented himself with less ambitious alterations. Baroque ceilings painted by Streater and J. M. Wright were installed in some of the rooms. A new palace gate and gallery leading to the guard chamber were erected – as well as the Volary Building on the river side, containing new lodgings for the King – wainscotted and painted white, or grained, and gilded. The new rooms for the King, which included a laboratory, library and bathroom, were completed in 1668.[5] Hugh May was responsible for their design. By 1670 Whitehall had been much improved, with new lodgings not just for the King but for several leading courtiers including the Earl of Lauderdale, the Earl of Peterborough, and the Earl of Rochester, as well as the succession of royal mistresses. Lady Castlemaine, the Duchess of Portsmouth, Duchesse Mazarin, Miss Stuart and Winifred Wells are all mentioned as being in residence at different times.[6] Various new works continued throughout the 1670s, splendid new furniture being ordered, the Tudor Chapel Royal being redecorated with much gilt, the Privy Garden extended, and another completely new range erected in 1682. In many ways Whitehall under Charles II enjoyed its liveliest period as the principal seat of the King and court. The King's lavish expenditure, the pomp and ceremonial, as well as the court etiquette and manners, favourably impressed even foreigners who were used to the magnificent court of Louis XIV, and contributed to an aura of splendour and dignity which partly made up for the irregularity of the architecture. The popularity of Charles himself, dining in public, walking in St James's Park with his spaniels, touching for the King's Evil, as well as the romantic intrigues of the court ladies, were all ingredients in the grand yet genial atmosphere of court life at Whitehall described by contemporary diarists such as Pepys, Evelyn and De Grammont.

When it became clear that a clean sweep of Whitehall would be difficult to achieve, Charles turned his attention to some of the other royal palaces, hoping that the same problems would not arise. At Newmarket, where Charles I's house had been destroyed by Colonel Okley in the Civil War, he built a small new house. At Greenwich he began an entirely new palace, following his marriage to Catherine of Braganza in 1661. The Queen's House had fortunately survived the Civil War relatively unscathed, but the Tudor buildings had been despoiled and were in a very dilapidated state, so were demolished. During the first decade of his reign Charles did more at Greenwich than at any other palace except Whitehall. The park was laid out anew in 1661–2 with formal avenues and elaborate grass terraces on the French model. The design for the parterre is reputed to have been made by the great French gardener Le Nôtre. Further gardening work was done in 1664 and 1665. John Webb supervised the enlargement of the Queen's House in 1662. The two bridge rooms were added

Greenwich. John Webb's
design for a new palace,
1664.

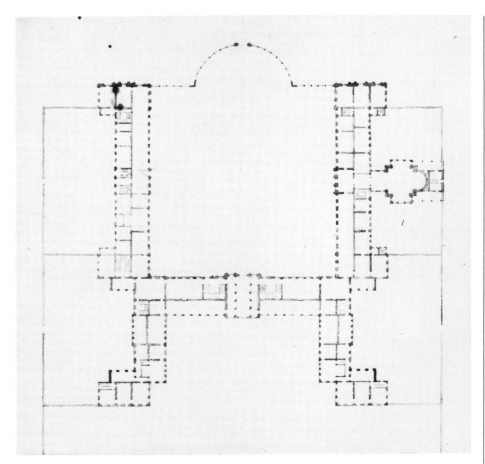

Greenwich. A ceiling
design by John Webb for
the new palace.

over the gaps in the middle of the sides, making it possible to rearrange the interior plan to form a 'King's Side' and a 'Queen's Side'. John Webb also provided plans for a completely new palace on the site of the old buildings. In one version the Queen's House was to become a centrepiece, enlarged by four corner pavilions on the model of a Palladian villa, each a self-contained lodging; the foundations for these were dug but nothing above ground was built. An alternative Webb scheme was for a three-sided palace with a domed centre facing the Thames. Work started on one of the flanking wings in January 1664. Over £44,000 was spent before the King's financial crisis of 1672 halted work, with just the shell completed. Webb's new range is long, low and monumental, with an attached Corinthian portico and chunky masonry details derived from Scamozzi. The decorative use of a giant order was something new in English architecture and ushered in a new monumentality, foreshadowing the English baroque style of Wren, Hawksmoor and Vanbrugh. The grand stone-faced architecture and dramatic layout, making the most of the riverside site, would have made Greenwich one of the noblest of the royal palaces. But it was never finished, let alone inhabited. James II suggested adapting the incomplete shell to some other purpose and in 1692, following the Battle of La Hogue, William and Mary converted it into the Royal Naval Hospital. It thus became part of a complex of classical buildings grander by far than any of the royal residences. The Queen's House became first the residence of the Ranger of Greenwich Park and then of the Governor of the Naval Hospital.[7]

Less ambitious works were done at various other palaces by Charles II. At Hampton Court he repaired the royal apartments (which like Whitehall had survived the Interregnum in the occupation of the Lord Protector) and dug the long canal in the park in 1668. At St James's he refurbished Inigo Jones's Catholic chapel for his wife, Catherine of Braganza. Wren added a baroque choir behind the altar (since removed), and the Queen built a Capuchin priory at her own expense for her Portuguese clergy. Somerset House was also refurbished. In 1665 Charles expressed the wish to build a 'noble house' at Woodstock, but this did not materialize and instead he bought Audley End in Essex, the largest Jacobean house in England, from the Earl of Suffolk; but he rarely stayed there and indeed never paid the full purchase price. The house was eventually returned to the Suffolk family. All this pales into insignificance compared to the remodelling of Windsor Castle to the design of Hugh May at a cost of over £130,000. Windsor and Holyrood alone were completed of Charles II's various building projects. Windsor was his favourite non-metropolitan palace and was of special significance to the restored monarchy. It was the only palace which could be effectively garrisoned, a not unimportant consideration after the recent upheavals. It housed St George's Chapel and St George's Hall, the headquarters of the Order of the Garter, England's prime order of chivalry and of special interest in the late seventeenth century, as is demonstrated by Elias Ashmole's history of the order and Lely's well-known drawings of the Garter procession. Windsor was also the burial place of the King's martyred father, Charles I, and it was intended to erect a suitable mausoleum to his memory, though nothing came of this.

Hugh May was appointed to supervise the work at Windsor in November 1673. The first phase – the provision of new state apartments for the King and Queen – was executed 1675–8. The second phase – the creation of a new royal chapel and St George's Hall – was begun in 1678. The structural work at Windsor was completed by 1680 and the interior decoration by 1684. The result was both ingenious and magnificent, and made the Upper Ward one of the most interesting baroque palaces in Europe. May's external work had a stripped down, almost austere, classical appearance, with round arched windows surrounded by simple concave Portland stone architraves, and a blocky massiveness to the parts

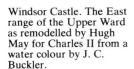

Windsor Castle. The East range of the Upper Ward as remodelled by Hugh May for Charles II from a water colour by J. C. Buckler.

which harmonized well with the character of the medieval fortress. The east front was more or less symmetrical, with four towers and a central two-branched staircase leading to the piano nobile. Much of the north side was taken up by a new block called the Star Building from the large gilded garter star which was its chief ornament. The interior was a rich contrast and formed the first and grandest sequence of baroque state apartments in England. It is tragic that so little survived the remodellings of George III and George IV. Only three lesser rooms still exist in anything like their original form, and even they have been more extensively altered than is at first apparent. But it is possible to study some of the lost rooms in the plates of W. H. Pyne's *Royal Residences*. As usual in England there were duplicated sets of state apartments for the King and the Queen. They were approached through a ground-floor vestibule with Ionic columns (some of the columns survive in the China Room) and niches in the walls containing antique busts. The Queen's Great Staircase, on axis with the entrance from the Upper Ward, was a remarkable ensemble with dramatic lighting partly through a glazed cupola in the domed ceiling and partly through an oval opening in the back wall revealing further spaces beyond. This gave an added dimension to the illusionistic paintings by Verrio. The King's Grand Staircase was at the east end of the Horn Court and approached through open arcades along the sides. The standard sequences of state rooms were arranged on the piano nobile round the Brick and Horn Courts. The King's Guard Chamber was partly top lit by a glazed octagonal lantern and gave access to the Audience and Privy Chambers, Drawing Room, Great Bedchamber and two closets. The Queen's suite contained a similar series of rooms and a Ball Room. The decoration in all these rooms was of striking novelty and set a fashion which was copied in most of the state apartments of private houses in late seventeenth-century England, with the result that Burghley or Chatsworth now give a better idea of the lost splendours of Windsor than the present appearance of the state rooms there. The ceilings were painted by Antonio Verrio, an Italian artist brought from Paris by the Duke of Montagu, Charles II's ambassador to Louis XIV. The walls were wainscotted, and festooned with amazing virtuoso carvings by Grinling Gibbons of fruit, flowers, fish and game, rather like Dutch still life paintings transformed into three dimensions. The gilding was by René Cousin, a Frenchman. The source of inspiration for the work in general was the France of Louis XIV, but the use of wood rather than coloured marbles gave Windsor a different character. Verrio's ceiling paintings were an important feature. By 1678 he had completed thirteen of them, all with fulsomely propagandist subjects – the Restoration of the Monarchy, the Re-establishment of the Church of England, Charles II triumphing over faction, and a general mingling of royal glory and classical mythology.

The climax of Charles II's reconstruction of Windsor was the redecoration of St George's Hall and the King's Chapel. The hall was painted by Verrio with feigned columns and grand historical setpieces showing the Black Prince's triumphal reception by Edward III, and Charles II in Garter robes enthroned in glory. The floor was paved with marble, and at one end was a glorious baroque throne, richly gilt and supported by carved figures of slaves, the work of Louis van Opstal and John Van der Stein. The overall scheme was symbolic of would-be absolutism as well as being a splendid setting for the Garter ceremonies. The throne had a short life, being removed by William III after the Glorious Revolution and replaced by a portrait of himself.

The adjoining chapel was even more spectacular. Its decoration formed a

Windsor Castle. The
Queen's Ballroom. The
ceiling by Antonio Verrio
has been destroyed.

Windsor Castle. St
George's Hall, before it
was reconstructed by
Wyatville, with mural and
ceiling paintings by Verrio.

remarkable unity. The walls and ceilings were covered with an integrated scheme of paintings by Verrio, depicting Christ's miracles behind a feigned marble colonnade along the walls and culminating in a huge painting of the Resurrection on the ceiling. Behind the altar was a small apse with a painting of the Last Supper framed by columns inspired by Bernini's *baldechino* in St Peter's, Rome, with gilded capitals and vast swags of flowers. Some of this ensemble was *tromple-l'oeil* painting and some of it carved and gilded wood. The semi-dome over the altar was open to reveal the gilded pipes of a concealed organ behind, a feature much admired by Evelyn. Round the lower parts of the walls were magnificent carved wooden stalls, their backs embellished with sprays of palm and laurel by Grinling Gibbons. Of this superb work all that now survives are some bits of the woodcarving splattered over the walls of the Waterloo Chamber.[8]

Concurrent with the reconstruction of Windsor Castle was Charles II's other major palace project carried through to completion, the rebuilding of Holyroodhouse in Edinburgh, the seat of the Scottish kings developed out of the guest house of Holyrood Abbey in the fifteenth and sixteenth centuries. The architect for this project was Sir William Bruce, 'the chief introducer of Architecture' to Scotland, who was appointed 'Surveyor-General and overseer of the King's Buildings in Scotland' from 1671 to 1678 specifically for the purpose of

Holyroodhouse, Edinburgh. It was reconstructed 1671–8 to the design of Sir William Bruce 'Surveyor-General and overseer of the King's Buildings in Scotland'.

rebuilding Holyrood. The whole project was probably conceived by the all-powerful Earl (later Duke) of Lauderdale (the L of the Cabal), who held sway over Scotland almost like a viceroy; Holyroodhouse was rebuilt as much as a political gesture as with any real intention of providing a house for the King to live in. In fact Charles never visited it, let alone stayed there for any period, nor did any of his successors before the twentieth century; apart from Bonnie Prince Charlie in 1745. In 1671 Holyroodhouse comprised an irregular group of buildings, of which the sixteenth-century north-west tower with its conical turrets was the principal feature. Assisted by Robert Mylne, the King's Master Mason in Scotland, Bruce formed a symmetrical front by building a duplicate tower to the south and linking the two by a lower balustraded range incorporating a Doric entrance portico. Behind this was built a new classical quadrangle with an arcaded ground floor and tiers of pilasters of French derivation. The whole exterior is thoroughly French in character, though the interior is more Anglo-Dutch with wainscotted walls, plaster ceilings, and painted decoration by Jacob de Wet, including 111 portraits of old Scottish kings in the Long Gallery, for which he was paid £120.[9]

Much of Charles's work at Windsor and Holyroodhouse was inspired by French architecture. His last and most francophile building project was not just stylistically inspired by Louis XIV's palaces but partly paid for out of the secret

Holyroodhouse.
The courtyard.

Winchester Palace. An
engraving of Wren's
original design showing the
open corner loggias and the
proposed domes.

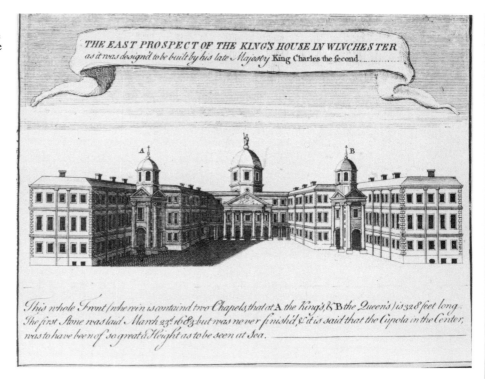

THE EAST PROSPECT OF THE KING'S HOUSE IN WINCHESTER
as it was design'd to be built by his late Majesty King Charles the second.

This whole Front (wherein is contain'd two Chapels, that at A the King's, & B the Queen's) is 328 feet long.
The first Stone was laid March 23rd 1683, but was never finish'd, & it is said that the Cupola in the Center,
was to have been of so great a Height as to be seen at Sea.

subsidies which Charles received from Louis. It was an entirely new royal palace
at Winchester, the ancient capital of England and well away from the watchful
eye of Parliament. It was intended as a 'hunting lodge', but was in fact big
enough for the whole court. Work began in 1682 with the demolition of most of
the remaining medieval palace and castle. Wren prepared designs for a stepped
plan reminiscent of Versailles. His first design was embellished with much pretty
French detail, but the executed design was simpler and stronger and influenced
by John Webb's work at Greenwich. In the centre was a giant portico and in the
corners open loggias. The façades were of brick, with Portland stone trim
including angle quoins and a balustraded parapet. The giant order of the portico
was Composite, while the lesser order of the loggias was Doric. Wren's design
shows domes on top, but they were never executed. The piano nobile was
devoted to five sets of state apartments – for the King, Queen, Duke and
Duchess of York, and the Duchess of Portsmouth (the King's current mistress).
Set in front of the palace at a lower level were the offices, arranged around an
outer courtyard reached from the main block by an elaborate flight of thirty
steps.

Work at Winchester progressed fast and the roof was completed by the time
of Charles II's death in 1685. The interior, however, was never fitted up and the
materials intended for it, including a gift of six white marble columns for the
main staircase from the Grand Duke of Tuscany, were dispersed. James II
halted work the moment he came to the throne in 1685, and the new palace was
abandoned, its windows boarded up and the shell left empty save for two
labourers and a dog. The land bought for a park was restored to the original
owners. Eventually the unfinished building was converted into barracks, and
burnt down in 1894.[10]

James II's short and politically disastrous reign might seem inappropriate for

Top: Winchester Palace. The entrance front after the fire of 1894.

Above: Winchester Palace. The exterior after the fire in 1894.

large-scale palace building, but in fact he was responsible for further substantial work at Whitehall in the years between 1685 and 1688. The Privy Garden range (south of the Banqueting House) was entirely rebuilt to provide new state rooms decorated with painted ceilings by Verrio and carving by Grinling Gibbons. A new grand staircase of stone with a wrought-iron balustrade was formed in the same range, giving access to the Banqueting House. In 1688 the part of the palace towards the river was also rebuilt to provide new lodgings for the Queen. Both the Privy Garden range, 200 feet long, and the Queen's Lodgings were designed by Wren in a relatively simple classical style of red brick with Portland stone dressings and with hipped roofs. These additions went a long way towards transforming Whitehall into a seemly classical palace, still with an irregular plan but composed of dignified and consistent architecture.

Whitehall Palace in the late seventeenth century, from St James's Park.

At one end of the Privy Garden range was the famous Catholic chapel designed by Wren. The Stuarts had always been ambivalent in their religion. James I's wife was rumoured to be a Catholic convert; Charles I and Charles II's wives were both Catholics, and Charles II himself became a Catholic on his deathbed. James II was an out and out Catholic, and came to the throne committed to the restoration of Catholicism in England. A new palace chapel in the baroque style was the expression of this aim. From documentary evidence and the bits which survive, it is possible to form an accurate impression of this splendidly appointed building. It was 80 feet long, with a simple brick and stone exterior harmonizing with the adjoining architecture. The interior rose the full height of the Privy Garden range and was, in Wren's words, 'decently adorned'. The floor was paved with marble, the walls and ceiling painted by Verrio at a cost of £1,250, and there was a good deal of gilding by René Cousin, who used 8,132 leaves of gold in the process. The ceiling was an oval dome frescoed with the Assumption. There were two organs by Renatus Harris, and the royal pew or gallery at the west end was opulently adorned with gilt baroque carvings. The *pièce de résistance*, however, was the carved marble alterpiece designed by Wren and executed by Grinling Gibbons and Arnold Quellin with bas reliefs and life-size angels on top. The large altar painting of the Nativity with adoring shepherds was by Benedeto Gennari and is now at Arundel Castle. Evelyn wrote on 29 December 1686:

I went to hear the music of the Italians in the new chapel, now first opened publicly at Whitehall for the Popish Service. Nothing can be finer than the magnificent marble work and architecture at the end, there are four statues, representing St John, St Peter, St Paul and the Church, in white marble, the work of Mr Gibbons, with all the carving and pillars of exquisite art and great cost. The altar-piece is the Salutation, the volto in fresco, the Assumption of the Blessed Virgin, according to their tradition, with our Blessed Savior, and a world of figures painted by Verrio.

Whitehall. Detail of the sculpture from James II's altarpiece (now at Burnham on Sea in Somerset).

The altarpiece was saved by being dismantled following the flight of James, and

Whitehall Palace in 1695

 Tudor

 Charles II and James II
1660–1688

 1 *King Street Gateway*
 2 *Part of Palace destroyed*
    by fire in 1691
 3 *The Stone Gallery*
 4 *The Volary Buildings*
 5 *The King's Apartment*
 6 *The Queen's Apartment*
 7 *Court*
 8 *Vane Room*
 9 *Privy Chamber*
10 *Presence Chamber*
11 *Chapel Royal*
12 *Great Hall*
13 *Guard Chamber*
14 *Gallery*
15 *The Pebble Court*
16 *Banqueting House*
17 *Gun Battery*
18 *Gallery*
19 *Roman Catholic Chapel*
20 *Chapel Court*
21 *Privy Gallery Range*
22 *The Privy Gallery*
23 *The Great Gate*
24 *The Great Court*
25 *Terrace Garden*
26 *Holbein Gateway*
27 *Privy Garden*

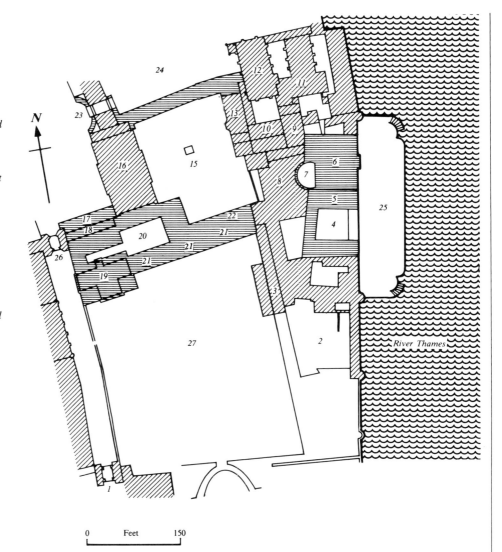

Whitehall. Wren's design
for the river terrace 280
feet long in front of the
Queen's apartments.

Overleaf: Whitehall in the
reign of James II, a bird's
eye view by Leonard Knyff.

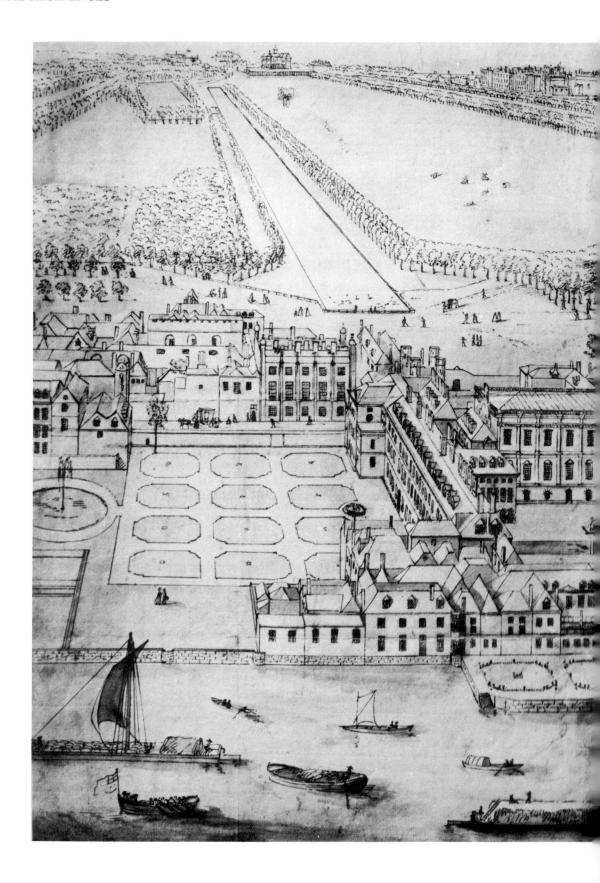

WHITHALL.

Whitehall. The ruins of the palace after the fire of 1698.

was given to Westminster Abbey by Queen Anne; the remaining fragments are now at Burnham-on-Sea in Somerset.[11]

Whitehall Palace did not long survive the deposition of James in 1688. A fire in 1691 caused serious damage, and was the precursor of an even more disastrous conflagration in 1698 which destroyed nearly everything except the Banqueting House, the two Tudor gateways, the Horse Guards, and a few subsidiary bits and pieces. Thanks to the exertions of Sir John Stanley the rich furniture of the palace was saved, 'not so much as a Curtain or stool missing'.[12] Some of it is now at Knole. Wren's office immediately set to work preparing plans for rebuilding the palace on a large scale with six courtyards and the Banqueting House incorporated in the centre. But once again nothing came of these proposals, mainly because William III's asthma made the low and damp riverside site insupportable. Parliament may also have been unwilling to grant money for rebuilding a palace so closely associated with attempts at royal absolutism by three successive monarchs. William had already made it clear that he found Whitehall uncongenial, though Mary had spent some time there during her husband's absences on the continent. She constructed a grand baroque terrace, 280 feet long, overlooking the river in front of the Queen's Lodgings. This was the last improvement at Whitehall before it was consumed in the flames.[13] Though Wren's designs for rebuilding Whitehall were not used, they nevertheless had an important impact on English architectural development. It was in the Office of Works at this time that the fully-fledged English baroque style was

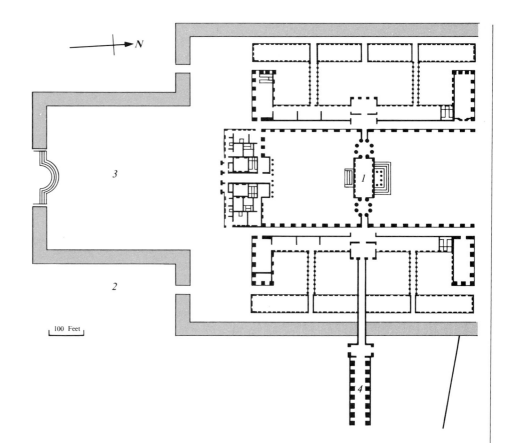

Whitehall Palace,
Sir Christopher Wren's
Plan for Rebuilding
in 1698.

1 *The Banqueting House*
2 *St James's Park*
3 *Garden*
4 *Covered way to the*
   Houses of Parliament

N

3

2

100 Feet

Whitehall. A design by
Wren for rebuilding the
palace after the fire.

Kensington Palace. The exterior showing the King's Gallery.

evolved, and many of Wren's ideas were taken up by Vanbrugh and Hawksmoor and exploited by them at Castle Howard and Blenheim.

Though nothing came of Whitehall, William and Mary were active elsewhere. As early as 1689 they had begun to rebuild Hampton Court and remodel Kensington as two very different palaces. Kensington was modest and homely – a private retreat of the King's; while Hampton Court was grand – the palace of the victorious monarch responsible for breaking the European ambitions of Louis XIV and for paving the way for the eighteenth-century triumph of England. The uses of the two palaces complemented each other. Hampton Court was a country palace intended for summer occupation, and was expensively and lavishly executed. Kensington, on the other hand, was a suburban retreat for use in winter, near enough to Westminster for the conduct of official business but away from the riverside damp and fog. Its architecture was utilitarian and cheap. William bought the Earl of Nottingham's 'villa' at Kensington in 1689 for £14,000. It was then a small Jacobean house. The King enlarged and rebuilt it piecemeal in four phases, resulting in an idiosyncratic plan and not very distinguished architecture. Evelyn thought it a 'sweete villa . . . yet a patched building'. The old house was kept and remodelled and four new bits added at each corner. The King's state rooms, and the approach to them, were constructed in 1689 in such a hurry that in November part of the new building which had just been roofed fell to the ground, killing seven or eight workmen. All William's building projects were undertaken at enormous speed, causing faults in their design as well as construction. The new entrance was rather oddly contrived via an elongated Doric porch and a long stone gallery leading to the great stairs. New enlarged Queen's apartments were added in 1695. The exterior of the King's Gallery is the only monumental feature at Kensington with brick pilasters and a parapet with urns. The design was produced by Wren's office and has been attributed to Hawksmoor. The rest of the palace is plainly domestic, built of stock brick with tall sash windows. William's interiors were plainly wainscotted. The Queen's apartments survive but the King's have been largely remodelled, though over the chimneypiece in the King's Gallery the large map of north-west Europe made by Robert Norden in 1694 survives in its original frame, as does the weather-vane superimposed on it to show the direction of the wind.[14] The gardens at Kensington were laid out by Henry Wise, £11,000 being spent between 1689 and 1696. Evelyn thought the results 'very noble, tho' not greate'. This work was continued by Queen Anne, who was also responsible for the magnificent baroque orangery 170 feet long, a masterpiece of cut brickwork with Doric columns. It was almost certainly designed by Vanbrugh and has all the splendour and assurance which the palace itself lacks. It cost £6,126.[15]

Kensington Palace. The inner court and entrance.

William and Mary's major building project was Hampton Court, and it was Wren's only full-scale palace, though even there the executed design is much reduced from his initial plans.[16] He had envisaged sweeping away all the Tudor buildings except Henry VIII's Great Hall. In the event, half the Tudor palace

was retained, and the juxtaposition of old and new work, so different in scale and architectural style, results in a far from satisfactory overall composition. The state rooms at Hampton Court are simpler than was originally envisaged by Wren and, with their plain wainscotting, they are much more sober than Charles II's at Windsor, let alone Louis XIV's marble and gilt enfilades at Versailles. Nevertheless the palace has many beauties, not least the Fountain Court with its arcaded walks and *oeil de boeuf* windows framed in carved lion skins hinting at the comparison of William III with Hercules, a theme which runs throughout the architecture.

The practical reason for rebuilding Hampton Court was to provide new royal apartments in duplicate sets for the King and Queen. But the new work was, on a less practical level, intended also to be a demonstration of triumph. Hampton Court was the palace of a victorious monarch, and the iconography of military glory runs through all its decoration. In style it is the ultimate expression of Anglo-Dutch design, with its staid enfilades of dark wainscotted rooms and its even façades executed in three different shades of red brick with crisply carved Portland stone dressings. It is on a larger scale than anything in William's native Holland, but is only half of what was at first envisaged. A further quadrangle, to form the river-entrance from the west, was intended to balance the east block containing the royal apartments, while the Tudor hall in the middle was to be the central feature of a grand new approach from the north. Altogether Wren

Hampton Court. The colonnade by Wren in the Clock Court.

Hampton Court. Wren's
Fountain Court.

produced four different schemes. In the event only the royal apartments were
reconstructed, on their old site and on a reduced scale. Wren also had to amend
his designs in various other ways not conducive to the finest architectural
effects. This was caused not so much by lack of money as by other practical
considerations. The King's desire for speed was probably the chief reason for
deciding on a partial rather than total reconstruction. The King's asthma also
meant that the piano nobile with the royal apartments had to be kept as low as
possible above the ground to reduce the number of steps which the King would
have to climb. This posed insuperable design problems, such as the curiously
botched tops of the courtyard arcades with dummy arches intended to conceal
the real first-floor level. Even worse is the absence of a proper plinth for the

Hampton Court Palace,
The State Apartments

■ Tudor buildings

▨ Wren's additions

1 *King's Kitchen*
2 *Tudor Kitchen*
3 *Great Hall*
4 *Great Watching
Chamber*
5 *Chapel Royal*
6 *Prince of Wales
Bedroom*
7 *Prince of Wales
Dressing Room*
8 *Prince of Wales
Presence Chamber*
9 *Prince of Wales
Staircase*
10 *Public Dining Room*
11 *Queen's Presence
Chamber*
12 *Queen's Guard
Chamber*
13 *Queen's Staircase*
14 *Clock Court*
15 *King's Staircase*
16 *King's Guard Room*
17 *King's First Presence
Chamber*
18 *King's Second Presence
Chamber*
19 *Audience Chamber*
20 *King's Drawing Room*
21 *King William III
Bedroom*
22 *King's Dressing Room*
23 *King's Writing Closet*
24 *Queen Mary's Closet*
25 *Queen's Gallery*
26 *King George II's
Private Chamber*
27 *King George II's
Dressing Room*
28 *Queen's Bedroom*
29 *Queen's Private
Chamber*
30 *Queen's Drawing Room*
31 *Private Dining Room*
32 *Queen's Audience
Chamber*
33 *Queen's Private Chapel*
34 *Fountain Court*
35 *Communication Gallery*
36 *Cartoon Gallery*

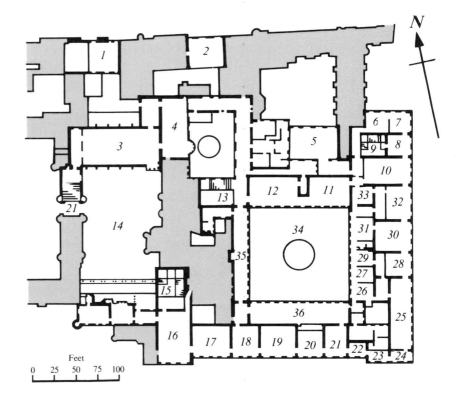

centrepiece of the east front, where the piano nobile window-sills rest not on solid stonework but immediately on top of the square heads of the ground-floor entrances with hardly any masonry in between, creating an unsatisfactory top heavy effect. The eye expects the whole carved stone centre to slide slowly to the ground at any moment.

Construction began in 1689 and by 1694 the exterior fabric was completed. Much of the craftsmanship is of superb quality, especially the stone-carving by Cibber and Gibbons, and the ironwork by Tijou. Following Queen Mary's death in 1694, William stopped the work. He shut up the palace and retired to Kensington, rather in the way that Richard II had abandoned Sheen after the death of his wife. He decided, however, to continue in 1699, and to fit out the state apartments. According to Wren, the 'Insides of these Rooms have long since been designed'. But the old designs were not followed in detail; much of the elaboration was omitted and a simpler finish substituted. William Talman supervised this work as well as fitting up lodgings for the courtiers. William Talman, with his son John, also made designs for a handsome little baroque trianon for William III at Thames Ditton, one and a half miles from Hampton Court, but it was not executed. In 1701 Verrio painted the ceilings of the King's rooms and the King's Staircase, the latter with the unusual subject of Julian the Apostate, who ranked in Whig mythology as a 'Symbol of toleration and

Hampton Court. The
King's Gallery.

Hampton Court.
Chimneypiece in William
III's Bedroom.

freedom'. Verrio's painting is not of very high quality, but it is good enough to serve its decorative purpose adequately. Altogether between 1699 and 1702, £43,155 14s 4d was spent on interior works at Hampton Court, in addition to £40,714 13s 6d spent on gardening in the same years.[17]

William III was an enthusiastic gardener and formed magnificent gardens in Holland at Het Loo and Huis ten Bosch. Hampton Court was his largest project. He filled in the west end of Charles II's canal pond in order to make a large semi-circular parterre beneath the east front of Wren's new block, while to the south, between the palace and the river, he made the Privy Garden with

Hampton Court. A corner chimneypiece designed in tiers to display some of Queen Mary's china.

Hampton Court. William Talman's unexecuted design for a trianon for William III at Thames Ditton.

symmetrical bosquets of clipped trees. The gardening itself was done by George London and the architectural supervision was by William Talman, while the design of the parterre with extravagant arabesques and little clipped pyramidal yews was provided by Daniel Marot, a Huguenot artist who had worked for William in Holland and had also designed china and a dairy for Queen Mary at Hampton Court. A great feature of the Hampton Court gardens are the architectural embellishments – the ironwork screens and gates by Tijou and the carved urns and similar ornaments by Edward Pearce and C. G. Cibber.[18] In 1699 a further ambitious project was undertaken to the north of the palace. This was the Bushy Park avenue, with its circular basin, 300 feet across, continuing the axis of Wren's proposed, but never realized, main approach to the palace.

All the works at Hampton Court were nearing completion when William died in 1701 as a result of his horse stumbling over a mole hill in the park at Hampton Court. His successor, Queen Anne, did very little to the palace apart from refurbishing the chapel in 1710, installing painted decoration by Sir James Thornhill, the Sergeant-Painter, and a carved wooden altarpiece designed by Wren and carried out by Grinling Gibbons. This was very much an expression of the Queen's pious High Church Anglicanism. Verrio also painted the Queen's Drawing Room with an allegory of England's sea power, but was subsequently paid off. He was told that 'there was no haste of any more painting'. Queen Anne did nothing in the gardens apart from simplifying Marot's parterre by removing some of the dwarf hedges, not for aesthetic reasons but because she did not like the smell of box. She also altered the radiating avenues in the park to improve their sporting potential. At her other palaces Queen Anne was equally unambitious. At Windsor she did not occupy Charles II's splendid state rooms but built a small lodge for herself on the south side of the castle precincts. In London, little effort was made to replace Whitehall, though further abortive

Kensington Palace. The
Orangery designed by
Vanbrugh for Queen
Anne.

plans for a new palace were prepared by John Talman. Instead, St James's was
patched up for the use of the court. A small block of new state rooms was
constructed to Wren's design on the south side overlooking St James's Park.
The exterior is frankly utilitarian – just plain stock brick walls with tall sash
windows. These state rooms still exist but were much enriched later, especially
under George IV, when lush stucco ceilings were inserted and masses of gilding
applied to everything, and again in 1866, when William Morris and Company
carried out a complete redecoration for the Office of Works. This small block
of state rooms at St James's marks the rather bathetic end of Stuart palace
building in England and is perfectly in keeping with the character of the stodgy
monarch whom Alexander Pope summed up in the brilliant couplet:

Here thou, Great Anna! whom three realms obey
do'st sometimes counsel take – and sometimes tea.

14. PREVIOUS PAGE: *The Charles II Dining Room, Windsor Castle.*

15. RIGHT: *Hampton Court. East façade by Wren.*

16. BELOW: *The Orangery, Kew.*

17. The King's Staircase,
Hampton Court.

18. The King's Drawing
Room, Kensington Palace.

19. The Saloon, Queen's
House. Aquatint from
W. H. Pyne Royal Residences
(1819).

VII

THE HANOVERIANS

The accession of the Hanoverian dynasty to the throne of Great Britain and Ireland in 1715, though politically expedient, was from the architectural point of view a disaster, and is the principal reason why London of all the major European capitals lacks a great eighteenth-century palace as one of its chief artistic treasures. There is no equivalent in England to the royal palaces of Madrid, Naples or Turin, the Winter Palace or Tsarskoe Selo, the Belvedere, Potsdam or Nymphenburg, Caserta, Aranjuez or Queluz. It is one of the ironies of history that Britain's attainment of world power status and unequalled economic prosperity should have coincided with the accession of a minor German Electoral dynasty to the English Crown and the architectural nadir of royal palace building in England. The Hanoverians had no English palace of any consequence. Whitehall had been burnt, Winchester was unfinished, Greenwich had become a naval hospital, Windsor was unoccupied, Hampton Court was half old-fashioned, even decayed, while Kensington was merely a rather dull suburban villa. The shabby old brick courts of St James's had to make do as the sole metropolitan palace of the Kings of England and as the centre of British social and political life. No serious effort was made to build a replacement in central London for the lost palace of Whitehall, though there were several schemes for the ambitious reconstruction of Kensington and St James's as well as for a completely new palace at Richmond. The archives at Windsor and elsewhere are full of unexecuted designs for palaces by Sir John Vanbrugh and James Gibbs, Sir Edward Lovatt Pearce and William Kent.

St James's was merely a 'nominal palace' and contemporaries were keenly aware of its inadequacy. Defoe wrote of it:

The Palace . . . though the winter receptacle of all the pomp and glory of this kingdom is really mean in comparison of the glorious Court of Great Britain. The splendours of the nobility, the wealth, and greatness of the attendants, and the real grandeur of the whole Royal Family, outdo all the Courts of Europe, and yet this palace comes beneath those of the most petty princes in it.

Nothing was done to remedy this state of affairs by the first two Georges, and John Gwynn writing in 1766 was even more forthright than Defoe. 'The palace of St James's', he wrote, 'is an object of reproach to the kingdom in general, it is universally condemned, and the meanest subject who has seen it, laments that his Prince resides in a house so ill-becoming the state and grandeur of the most

Kensington. Sir John
Vanbrugh's unexecuted
plan for a new palace for
George I.

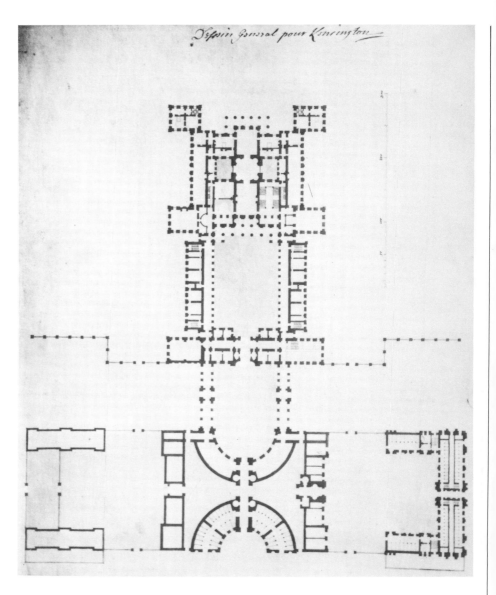

powerful and respectable monarch in the universe.'[1] The contrast between the
splendour of the great private houses of the Whig aristocracy – Stowe,
Chatsworth, Castle Howard or Blenheim – and St James's, more like one of the
smaller and more old-fashioned Cambridge colleges, struck everybody.

The failure to build an adequate replacement for the lost palaces of the
ancient Kings of England at a time which is generally regarded as one of the
greatest periods of English architectural achievement was largely due to the
character of the first two Hanoverian kings. Neither of them cared much for
England or for art. Their own palace at Herrenhausen in Hanover with its
French-style formal gardens continued to come first in their affections. George
I had a very strong distaste for British public life and spent so little time in
England that a satirical poster was pinned to the gate of St James's: 'It is
reported that His Hanoverian Majesty deigns to visit his British Dominions for
three months in the Spring.' And Sir Robert Walpole's government was afraid
that the King's failure to play his role in public life would lead to the less

gloomy Prince of Wales becoming the centre of a rival political faction. The King was shy, his taste was drab, and he could not speak English. Moreover he hated crowds and ceremony. He and his prime minister, Walpole, discussed government business in schoolboy Latin. George I found the English court, with its ingrained traditions and jealously guarded perquisites, totally irrational. He grumbled: 'The first morning after my arrival at St James's I looked out of the window and saw a park, with walks, and a canal, which they told me, were mine. The next day Lord Chetwynd, the Ranger of my Park, sent me a fine brace of carp, out of my canal, and I was told I must give five guineas to Lord Chetwynd's servant for bringing me my own carp, out of my canal, in my own park.'[2] He wanted to have in England the simple court life which he enjoyed in Hanover and refused to be dressed formally in leisurely stages by Peers of the Realm. Instead he was dressed privately by his own personal German servants whom he brought over from Hanover and who protected his privacy. He dined privately, too, and altogether lived more like a recluse in 'his bare palace of St James's' than like a King of England.

While George I hated public life and the formality of the English court, George II was simply philistine, though he did enjoy the formal trappings of royalty more than his father. His lack of interest in his palaces and art treasures comes across clearly in Lord Hervey's feline memoirs of the court. Hervey, for instance, describes a revealing incident when he and Queen Caroline attempted to improve the arrangement of the rooms at Kensington. 'My Lord', said the King in heavy German accents, 'I have a great respect for your taste in what you understand, but in pictures I beg leave to follow my own. I suppose you assisted the Queen with your fine advice when she was pulling my house to pieces and spoiling all my furniture. Thank God, at least she has left the walls standing. As for the Vandykes, I do not care whether they are changed or no; but for the picture with the dirty frame over the door, and those three nasty children (Van Dyck's beautiful study of the family of Charles I) I will have them taken away . . .'

The Hanoverians' legendary hatred of father for son also mitigated against any sort of long-term architectural enterprise. George I and George II's dislike for each other was strong enough, but was eclipsed by that of George II for his eldest son, Frederick, Prince of Wales. The King called Frederick the 'greatest ass and the greatest liar, and the greatest canaille and the greatest beast in the whole world', while Queen Caroline expressed her opinion of her son more succinctly: 'Fred is a nauseous little beast.'

On arriving in England George I chose Hampton Court and Kensington as his summer palaces and ignored Windsor, which languished unoccupied for most of the eighteenth century. At Hampton Court the new King did very little. The ceiling of his bedchamber was painted by Verrio in 1715, and Vanbrugh completed some rooms for the occupation of the Prince and Princess of Wales in his distinctive style, with boldly modelled ceilings and massive marble chimneypieces. In 1716 Vanbrugh also produced a scheme for a grand northern entrance to the palace on the Bushy Park axis contrived by Wren, but ingeniously arranged so as to retain the best of the surviving parts of the Tudor palace. The Great Hall was to form a centrepiece flanked by long, dramatically arcaded wings terminating in pavilions like a larger-scale version of Seaton Delaval. It is sad that this dramatic scheme was not carried out, as it would have helped to marry the two disparate portions of the palace, Wren's baroque block and the Tudor Gothic courts, into one grand picturesque whole.[3]

George I was more active at Kensington, which he preferred to Hampton Court because it was less formal. It was reported to be much out of repair: 'the old front . . . being much crakt'. Vanbrugh made ambitious plans for rebuilding the entire palace on the scale of Blenheim. Only Wren's gallery was to be retained as the central feature of the south front flanked by boldly projecting new pavilions. Two arcaded hemicycles linked by a towering gatehouse formed the outer entrance, leading to a sequence of courtyards in which Vanbrugh 'had exercised all his genius for architectural pomp and circumstance'.[4] Nothing came of this either. George I did not want a great palace, merely a surburban retreat from London. He confined himself to the reconstruction of the decayed central part of Kensington, the original Nottingham House, to create three new state rooms on the first floor, a drawing room, the Cupola Room and the Privy Chamber. The architecture and decoration of this new work marked something of a revolution in English taste, the swing away from the baroque of Wren and Vanbrugh to the Palladianism of the new Whig establishment, Colen Campbell, William Kent and Henry Flitcroft.

The Sergeant-Painter, Thornhill, was passed over and the decoration of these rooms was entrusted in 1721 to William Kent, a protégé of Lord Burlington, newly returned from Rome, who was to become the unofficial designer to all the royal family for twenty years. Being young and inexperienced, Kent was cheaper than the infinitely more accomplished Thornhill. Kent's work pleased George I's undiscriminating taste and he was immediately commissioned to carry out a general redecoration of the royal apartments at Kensington where, between 1722 and 1727, at least £17,000 was spent on alterations. The architect of these new rooms is not known. Wren was dismissed from the Office of Works in 1718 and was replaced by William Benson, who favoured the new Palladian style. It has been suggested that one of the key Palladians like Colen Campbell may have been responsible for the alterations at Kensington; certainly the Cupola Room is among the earliest Palladian ensembles in England. It is a cube of 37 feet and was intended for evening entertainments. Much of the decoration is painted in *trompe-l'oeil*, including the octagonal blue and gold coffering of the domed ceiling, the fluted pilasters, and the trophies of gold and brown on the walls. The beautifully proportioned Ionic doorcases are of white marble, and in niches around the walls are gilded statues of gods and goddesses. Kent's painting was condemned by some contemporaries as being too flat and the whole scheme by others as being vulgar. But it should be remembered that it was designed to be seen by candlelight. The gilding and the *trompe-l'oeil* would have been far more effective in the evening than in the harsher light of day. W. H. Pyne, the early nineteenth-century topographical artist, grasped the point when he wrote: 'The cupola room . . . with all its defects exhibits a rich and picturesque appearance; for though it wants unity and propriety, it is bold in its parts and calculated to produce a variety of light and shadow when illuminated by the chandeliers.'[5]

Kent's other ceilings at Kensington vary in quality. That in the Drawing Room sports a complimentary, if absurd, allegory of Mars and Minerva in which Mars is wearing the Order of the Garter. The handling of this grandiose subject shows the artist at his most incompetent. More original and interesting are the ceilings of the King's Bedchamber, the Presence and Council Chambers, which were painted in 1724 with 'grotesque' work inspired by ancient Roman painting, and the Raphael Loggia. With Kent's similar ceiling in the Parlour at Rousham, they are among the earliest examples of this neo-antique decoration in Europe.

Kensington. The King's
Gallery as redecorated by
William Kent.

Kent's designs of scrolls and medallions are attractive, and the colouring warm,
with the bright reds and dark blues, enriched with gilding, showing up well
against white grounds. The King's Gallery was given a similar painted 'grotesque'
ceiling as part of a unified new scheme of decoration worked out by Kent. He
painted and gilded the wainscot and designed new doorcases, chimneypieces,
pedestals, and side tables with marble tops.

The last of the palace interiors to be decorated by Kent was the King's
Staircase. There he covered the walls with elaborate Venetian-influenced
trompe-l'oeil paintings on canvas. The lower storey was painted simply with
trophies within panels, but the upper part was treated as an open colonnade
behind which a curious medley of bystanders watch the visitors mounting the
stairs. They include Yeomen of the Guard, courtiers, 'Peter the Wild Boy' (a
defective creature brought to England in 1726 and presented to George I),
Ulrich, a dwarf, 'commonly called the Young Turk, in his Polonese dress as he
waited on the late King George', and two Turkish grooms, Mehemet and
Mustapha. The ceiling above is designed to give the idea of an open dome, with
further spectators including Kent himself and an actress, who is reputed to have
been his mistress, looking down on the stairs.[6]

At St James's Vanbrugh also made exciting plans for large-scale reconstruction of the whole palace as well as a less ambitious scheme for building a new

Opposite: Kensington. The King's Staircase painted by William Kent.

south front overlooking St James's Park.[7] But neither scheme was taken seriously by the King and he restricted all work at the palace to minor piecemeal alterations, mainly of a backstairs variety, including the fitting up of apartments for his two fat German mistresses, the Countess of Schulenberg (later the Duchess of Kendal) and 'Madame Kilmansack'. The only notable alterations were the construction of new offices impinging on corners of the old Tudor courts and including new wine cellars and laundry and a large two-storeyed kitchen designed by Vanbrugh.

The only new work undertaken in the course of George I's reign was the White Lodge or New Park Lodge at Richmond. The New Park at Richmond on the other side of the town from the Old Deer Park and site of Henry VII's palace on the Kew side (with which it should not be confused) had been created by Charles I and stocked with deer for hunting. George I enjoyed the sport there but found the absence of a hunting lodge inconvenient and at the end of his reign gave orders for one to be built. The design was approved in the winter of 1726–7 and work started immediately. The architect was Roger Morris, the protégé of the 9th 'architect' Earl of Pembroke who was himself involved in the design. It is a coolly elegant five-bay Palladian villa, containing four rooms on the piano nobile with bedrooms above and offices below. The exterior was faced in white Portland stone which gave it its name, and the chief feature is an attached Tuscan portico on the garden front, raised above a rusticated plinth.

Richmond. White Lodge, a hunting box designed by Roger Morris for George I, 1726.

Hampton Court. The range between the Fountain and Clock Courts rebuilt by William Kent in 1732.

The house was not intended for regular habitation but mainly for dining and resting after a day's hunting. George I died in 1727, while work was still in progress, and the lodge was completed by George II for his wife Queen Caroline, who used it frequently and in whose memory the avenue on the Richmond side is still called the Queen's Ride.[8]

George II, after his accession to the throne, continued to reside at Hampton Court in the summer. He made various alterations to the palace, rather more than is immediately apparent, for he kept to the Tudor Gothic style at the behest of Sir Robert Walpole, who wanted the new work to harmonize with the old.[9] The elevation of the Fountain Court Range towards the Clock Court was rebuilt in 1732 with a new central gateway, to replace the old range which had fallen into ruin. It has convincing octagonal turrets at the corners and a pointed Gothic archway. This was designed by William Kent, who was also responsible for the suite of new rooms inside intended for the occupation of the Duke of Cumberland. Though small they are handsomely appointed, with richly stuccoed ceilings and carved marble chimneypieces. Following the death of Queen

Caroline, George II left Hampton Court and the palace was never again used by the royal family. George III hated it because it reminded him of the blood-curdling family quarrels of his youth and one especially painful occasion when his irascible grandfather had boxed his ears. When a fire broke out in part of the palace in 1770 he told Lord Hertford 'that he shou'd not have been sorry if it had been burnt down'.[10] Nevertheless he kept the fabric in good repair; for example, when the main gatehouse turned out to be in danger of collapse it was rebuilt in 1770–72 in the old style, thus maintaining the conservative approach to the Tudor work begun by William Kent. Much of the palace was later divided into 'Grace and Favour' apartments, becoming in the words of William IV 'the quality poor house', and the state rooms and grounds were opened to the public by Queen Victoria. An amusing reminder of the years when the palace was left empty and forlorn are the names of schoolboys with eighteenth-century dates amateurishly carved into the stone steps of the lower flights of the King's Staircase.

George II did no new structural work to Kensington Palace but was responsible for extensive improvements in the gardens carried out under Charles Bridgeman's direction. These included the creation of Rotten Row and the Serpentine in Hyde Park, as well as various new garden buildings.[11] After his death Kensington, like Hampton Court, ceased to be occupied by the King and

St James's Palace. The Colour Court showing how the Tudor buildings were patched up and adapted to serve as a metropolitan palace for the Hanoverians.

was divided into small residences for lesser members of the royal family. At St James's, too, very little was done beyond routine repairs, the reconstruction of the Royal Mews at Charing Cross (now the site of the National Gallery) to William Kent's design, and the addition of a library for Queen Caroline on the Green Park side of the palace. The Queen was more intelligent and cultivated than her husband, as this library demonstrated. It was designed by William Kent and was a single-storeyed, almost free-standing double cube of 60 feet by 30 feet. It was of considerable architectural merit and it is to be regretted that it was demolished in 1825. Its appearance, however, is recorded in contemporary drawings. The interior was extremely handsome, with a deeply coved ceiling and the bookcases marshalled in arched recesses with marble busts by Rysbrack on brackets between. At either end were carved marble chimneypieces with scrolly pedimented overmantels containing portraits.

William Kent continued to be much employed both by the Queen and also by Frederick, Prince of Wales, who, unlike his father, was something of a connoisseur and patron. Horace Walpole noted that Kent was 'not only consulted for furniture, glasses, tables, chairs, etc. but for plate, for a barge, for a cradle'.[12] The royal barge was made in 1732 for Frederick, Prince of Wales in a fanciful Venetian style with rich carving by James Richard and gilding by Paul Pettit. This barge is now preserved in the National Maritime Museum; the 'mighty pretty cradle', however, has disappeared. It was commissioned by Frederick for his younger son Prince Henry Frederick, Duke of Cumberland, who was born in 1745.

The palatial dreams of George II were not centred on St James's, Kensington or Hampton Court but on Richmond where, in 1719, as Prince of Wales, he had

William Kent's design for a royal barge for Frederick Prince of Wales.

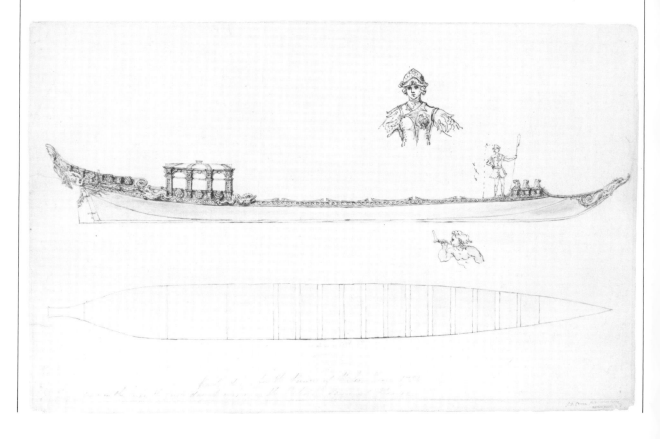

Right: St James's. A chimneypiece designed by William Kent for Kensington Palace.

St James's. Queen Caroline's Library. (Demolished 1825.)

Richmond. The wooden model showing William Kent's unexecuted design for a new palace for George II.

Opposite: St James's. Chimneypiece by William Kent from the Queen's Library, now in the Throne Room.

acquired the house of the Jacobite Duke of Ormonde who had fled the country in 1715. This house occupied the site of the ancient royal palace which had been largely destroyed in the Civil War. After the Restoration it had been given by Charles II to his brother, the Duke of York, who had thought of building a new palace there to Wren's design. In the event the ruins were patched up by William III in 1694 as a 'lodge', and after his death leased to Ormonde for his official residence as Ranger of Richmond Park. When it came to George II, the house had a symmetrical red brick façade concealing an irregular plan, and was described at the time as being 'a perfect Trianon'. Its chief attractions were the riverside position and the gardens which made it a pleasant summertime retreat. The building itself was rather ramshackle. According to Lord Hervey, what was said in one room could be heard in the next because the walls were so thin.

George II, after he came to the throne, considered replacing Richmond Lodge with a new house on a grander scale. Sir Edward Lovett Pearce, the Surveyor-General of Ireland, submitted plans for a Palladian 'lodge' in the style of Colen Campbell. He proposed a square of 173 feet with a logical plan of duplicated state rooms for the King and Queen on either side of a grand staircase. The design was 'confined to conveniency and proper use without magnificence, ornament or great expense' at the request of the King. Nothing came of Pearce's scheme, however, and soon afterwards the ubiquitous William Kent produced a full-scale pear-wood model for a grander palace on the model of Holkham and Chiswick.[13] Nothing came of this splendid proposal either, and instead George II contented himself with some small-scale alterations to the existing house and the addition of a library at the back for Queen Caroline, whose dower house Kew Lodge became.

In the 1730s she spent large sums of money on the gardens, which were landscaped on a generous scale by Charles Bridgeman, appointed 'Master Gardiner to His Majesty' in 1728.[14] Gardening was Caroline's overriding passion, and she, rather than her husband, had been the initiator of the improvements in Kensington Gardens and was chiefly responsible for the royal patronage of Bridgeman. The layout at Richmond ran to hundreds of acres and included a forest walk and a riverside terrace threaded through a variety of scenery designed 'to help nature' and dotted with ornamental buildings including a hermitage, dairy, domed temple, and 'Merlin's Cave'. The latter was inhabited by a curious assembly of wax effigies – the magician himself, his secretary, Elizabeth of York, the goddess Minerva, Elizabeth I and her nurse, attended by one live poet, Stephen Duck, a protégé of the Queen. The 'Cave' and the hermitage are both known to have been designed by William Kent, so he was probably responsible for the other buildings too. Horace Walpole singled out Bridgeman's work at Richmond for special praise: 'As (Bridgeman's) reputation gained footing, he ventured further, and in the royal garden at Richmond dared to introduce cultivated fields and even morsels of a forest appearance, by the sides of those endless and tiresome walks, that stretch'd out of one into another without intermission.'

Queen Caroline's Richmond Lodge and gardens should not be confused with the adjoining Kew Gardens. They were not combined to make one garden until the reign of George III and only became the Royal Botanic Gardens in 1841. Kew was the domain of Frederick, Prince of Wales, who held court there from 1729 till his premature death in 1751, whereupon it became the dower house of his widow, Augusta, Dowager Princess of Wales, the mother of George III. As has been noted already, Frederick was the first of the Hanoverians to show any concern for art. He formed an interesting collection of Italian paintings, was a patron of music, and something of a pioneer in promoting the rococo style in England. Between 1731 and 1735 he built an elegant new lodge at Kew called 'Kew Palace', or the White House. It was William Kent's first architectural achievement of any consequence at the time he was turning from painting to architecture. The highly gilded and richly decorated rooms with chimneypieces by Rysbrack and furniture by Kent, and the statue-filled vistas of Kew, presented a spectacle of tasteful splendour not equalled at that time in any other of the royal residences.

The garden round the White House was small at first but was considerably altered in the 1750s when various features were added: Mount Parnassus, an antique aqueduct, the 'India House', and the 'House of Confucius'. The architect of these structures is not known, but it may have been Sir William Chambers, though this attribution is questionable.[15] Following Frederick's death, his widow continued to enlarge and improve the gardens till they were among the finest of their type in England on account of their elaborate buildings and also their exotic planting. Chambers was appointed architect to the Princess in 1757 and he was responsible for the design of most of the new garden buildings. The garden as remodelled became an enclosed, inward-looking landscape surrounded by belts of trees which cut off any external prospects. This wooded framework was dotted with temples and ornaments which provided the principal objects of interest. The central flat area was simply treated as 'lawns' grazed by sheep and variegated by an L-shaped lake. Although now greatly altered and replanted, with many buildings demolished, just enough survives to suggest something of the original character of this princely Arcadia; not just buildings like the pagoda, ruined arch, orangery and temples of Bellona and Pan, but also some of the original planting including a magnificent Chinese wisteria planted in 1761 and a ginko planted in 1762, one of the earliest in England.

Kew. The Pagoda designed by Sir William Chambers for the Dowager Princess of Wales 1761.

The appearance of the garden in its heyday is recorded in Sir William Chambers's *Plans, Elevations, Sections and Perspective Views of the Gardens and Buildings at Kew* published in 1763. The orangery, dated 1761, near the site of the house was the largest of the classical garden buildings and is a sober, masculine design of brick, stuccoed to resemble channelled stonework, with tall round-arched windows and pedimented end pavilions. The Temple of the Sun, also built in 1761, was the earliest imitation in England of the Temple of the Sun at Baalbec and pre-dated that at Stourhead. The Physic Garden, or Exotic Garden, which foreshadowed the eventual use of the whole garden for botanic collections, was planted by William Aiton, Princess Augusta's gardener, under the supervision of Lord Bute, with the 'compleatest and best collection of

Kew. The Ruined Arch leading to the Wilderness.

curious Plants in Europe'. The more delicate plants were housed in the Great Stove, a large glasshouse 114 feet long designed by Chambers in 1761 (demolished in 1861). The adjoining flower garden had a fretted chinoiserie aviary in the centre, and nearby was an octagonal chinoiserie menagerie. Further out was the Doric Temple of Bellona, and the older House of Confucius was re-sited in the same area. Beyond was the Temple of Victory (demolished), which commemorated the Battle of Minden in August 1759, a battle in which George II had personally led a charge, the last English monarch to take part in warfare. The ruined Roman arch gave access to the Wilderness, where the Alhambra (demolished), Pagoda and Mosque (demolished) combined to create a powerful Eastern effect. The Alhambra, a colourful exotic design painted in red, yellow and blue, was designed in 1759 by J. H. Müntz, an artist of German-Swiss origin who for a time was a protégé of Horace Walpole's, but was dismissed by him 'for some amorous misdemeanor'. The Mosque was by Chambers, and seems to have been inspired by the engraved reconstructions of Turkish architecture published in Vienna by Fischer von Erlach. It had an enchanting interior, with green-painted stucco palm trees surrounding a domed ceiling painted by Richard Wilson to resemble a sky. The Pagoda, the principal survivor at Kew, was designed by Chambers and is 160 feet high. It is the most ambitious chinoiserie garden structure in Europe. It seems rather austere now

Above left: Kew. The
Temple of the Sun by
Chambers. (Demolished.)

Above right: Kew. The
Temple of Bellona by
Chambers.

Kew. The Temple of
Aeolus by Chambers.

with its bare stock brick walls, but originally it was covered all over with glittering glazed tiles and the roof ridges were decorated with eighty brightly coloured iron dragons. The Pagoda must always have been the major attraction of the gardens, but there were many other substantial buildings, all now demolished, such as the Gothic Cathedral by Müntz with a façade 50 feet wide, an open-air Gallery of Antiques with marble reliefs and statues depicting the Seasons and the Arts carved by Joseph Wilton, the Ionic Temple of Arethusa built in 1758, the domed octagonal Temple of Solitude and the Temple of Peace, with a splendid Ionic portico which was never completed and soon demolished.[16]

Few English gardens could boast an array of temples as fine as Kew's and, with its planting by Aiton, it was considered the epitome of 'all that English taste has been capable of producing, most magnificent and most variegated'. It is sad that so little is left of what was the finest royal *jardin anglais* in Europe. To envisage something of the effect now it is necessary to go to Russia and walk round Tsarskoe Selo, where a similar English-style landscape garden crammed with temples still survives. Kew Gardens, the Palladian White Lodge at Richmond (New) Park and some rooms and decoration by William Kent are the only notable contributions of the first three generations of the Hanoverians to the history of royal palace-building in England. It is not an impressive achievement compared to that of a Duke of Bedford, a Marquess of Rockingham or a Marquess of Buckingham. It was left to George III and George IV to try to make good the deficiency.

VIII

GEORGE III

The accession of a young King in 1760 was widely welcomed by British artists and architects who had been starved of royal patronage during the previous two reigns and looked for much from George III, who was known to be something of a connoisseur and who had been taught architectural drawing by Sir William Chambers.[1] The elaborate symbolism of the State Coach, completed in 1762, summarizes the aspirations of the monarch and his subjects at the opening of the new reign. It is a triumphal chariot embellished with military trophies in celebration of the English victories in the Seven Years War and optimistic allusions to the Arts of Peace: 'Industry and Ingenuity giving a cornucopia to the genius of England' and 'the liberal Arts and Sciences protected'. This magnificent carved, gilded and painted rococo object was designed by Sir William Chambers, the painted panels were by Cipriani and the carving by Joseph Wilton, while Samuel Butler was responsible for the coachwork. The general form follows the fashionable model of contemporary French coaches, while the gilded palm trees and lions' masks, the feathered helmets and tritons, the tridents and imperial fasces, the three genii of England, Scotland and Ireland supporting the royal insignia all combine to form a rich allegorical celebration of the world-wide power of the English Crown and epitomize the triumphalist mood at the opening of the new reign. If this was the new coach commissioned by the King, what would his palaces be like?[2]

As a demonstration of his architectural intent George III created a new post, 'Architect of Works', in 1761 which was shared by the two leaders of the profession, Robert Adam and Sir William Chambers, the latter receiving the lion's share of the work. Adam did very little for George III, just an orrery, one ceiling and one chimneypiece at Buckingham House, but in the 1760s and 1770s Chambers made designs for a new royal residence at Richmond, for the Royal Observatory there, for remodelling Buckingham House and for the Queen's Lodging at Windsor. In the end the scheme for a new classical style royal residence at Richmond came to nothing, though at least four different sets of plans were prepared and a start was actually made on building work. In October 1761 Count Frederick Kielmansegge reported that the King had 'decided to begin the building of an entirely new palace' at Richmond. This first scheme, however, was deferred by the purchase and remodelling of Buckingham House, following the King's marriage to Charlotte of Mecklenburg-Strelitz, in order to provide a comfortable modern residence in London close to St James's Palace,

The state coach designed by Sir William Chambers for George III.

which was considered too antiquated to live in, but where the State Rooms continued to be used for court functions: balls, levees, drawing-rooms, royal marriages and christenings.

When expenditure on Buckingham House began to decrease, Sir William Chambers was asked to make revised plans for the Richmond palace which was intended to be the King's chief country house and to replace the antique inconveniences of Hampton Court and of Windsor. Numerous drawings for this project survive in the Royal Library at Windsor, and a wooden model (destroyed in 1922) was made by Benoni Thacker in 1765. The estimated cost was £89,320, and the old-fashioned Palladian plans show a compact block, 338 feet by 225 feet, with corner pavilions and a Corinthian portico on the model of Holkham but larger. 'Capability' Brown was commissioned to landscape the gardens intended to form a setting for this new palace. Queen Caroline's fussy rococo layout with its grottoes and twisting paths was cleared away to create unencumbered sweeps and spacious lawn and simpler plantations:

To Richmond come; for see, untutor'd Brown
Destroys the wonders which were once their own;
Lo! from his melon-ground the peasant slave
Has rudely rush'd and levell'd Merlin's Cave,
Knock'd down the waxen wizard, seized his wand,
Transformed to lawn what late was fairy-land,
And marr'd with impious hand each sweet design
Of Stephen Duck and good Queen Caroline.[3]

Though the work on the garden progressed, Chambers's second scheme for the palace followed its predecessor into oblivion and in 1769 he prepared a third design, which was exhibited at the Royal Academy that summer. The foundation stone was laid in 1770 and the vaulted ground floor of the central block, 140 feet square, rose rapidly on a site midway between the Queen's cottage and the Observatory, looking down over the river. But then work suddenly stopped again. Thomas Worsley wrote to Chambers on 19 January 1773: 'Pray how do you go at Kew, does Richmond stand still? What a pity he cannot go on with so small a design. If it were a grand *Caserta* I should not be surprised, but so modest an undertaking to stop or go on so slow is hard.' The scheme was not, however, totally dead, for in August 1775 Chambers produced yet a further revised design for a more grandiose Palladian scheme, with a nine-bay centre block incorporating the ground floor already erected and linked by quadrant colonnades to corner pavilions each three-bays square, similar to James Paine, Matthew Brettingham's and Adam's recently completed scheme at Kedleston in Derbyshire. The façades of this final version of the Richmond classical design reflected George III's conservative taste and Chambers's academic approach, showing the influence of Inigo Jones's New Gallery at Somerset House but livened up with pretty Frenchified detail, the fruit of Chambers's visit to Paris.[4]

This scheme too floundered, and in the event George III's architectural achievement at Richmond was confined at this stage to the Royal Observatory built in 1768, also to Chambers's design, in order to enable the King to watch the Transit of Venus the following year, an event which aroused widespread interest in scientific circles throughout Europe. George III was the first British king to be taught science as part of his education and he maintained an interest in the subject throughout his life. He placed the Observatory initially under the charge of Demainbray, but in 1782 Herschal, from whom the King had bought at least five telescopes for 600 guineas each, was appointed Astronomer Royal. The Richmond Observatory is a delightful architectural ensemble, with an octagonal centre containing the principal rooms on both floors, each fitted with glazed cabinets for the display of minerals and scientific instruments which included the silver orrery designed by Robert Adam (now in the History of Science Museum at Oxford). In these elegantly utilitarian surroundings the King spent many happy hours testing the elaborate clocks which he collected and which were his special enthusiasm. He kept at the Observatory a register of their accuracy, written in his own hand.[5]

The King's failure to build a new country palace at Richmond was not just due to lack of money, because during his lifetime he managed to spend a very large sum of money on his various abortive architectural projects. It was more the result of a basic ambivalence. While toying with the idea of building a new palace, even making a large number of designs in his own hand for a series of

Richmond. Sir William Chambers's third design for a new royal palace for George III.

Richmond. The Royal
Observatory designed by
Sir William Chambers for
George III.

Richmond. Obelisk
connected with the
observatory and used for
measuring London's time.

dull Palladian piles, he did not really want to live in one. He preferred small
private houses, and the most accurate reflection of his taste was Buckingham
House in London, which he reconstructed between 1762 and 1774 at a cost of
£73,000, part of which sum was spent on making the existing building less
palatial and less imposing. His need for a new London residence fortunately
coincided with a dispute over the irregularities of the lease of Buckingham
House, which led to the Crown Estate acquiring the building for £28,000. It had
been built in the late seventeenth century by William Winde for John Sheffield,
Duke of Buckingham, and was then more of a country house on the edge of
London than a town house, and to some extent it has retained this character
ever since because of its parkland setting, despite the gigantic expansion of
London to the west in the past three centuries. The baroque red brick exteriors

of the original design were long out of fashion when George III bought the house, and so it was decided to encase them in smooth new brick, omitting the pilasters from the corners and hiding the basement storey by raising the forecourt. Tijou's grand iron screens in front were replaced by simpler railings symbolizing George III's unpretentious taste. The resulting house was a villa rather than a palace and emphatically a private residence of the royal family, not the seat of the court, which remained St James's, resulting in the anomaly whereby foreign ambassadors are still accredited to the Court of St James two centuries later. The King's rooms at Buckingham House were fitted up neatly but, by royal standards, extremely plainly. There were, for instance, no carpets, as the King thought them unhealthy. John Adams, the American Minister to England, who visited Buckingham House in 1783, was struck by the simplicity of the King's rooms: 'In every apartment of the whole house, the same taste, the same judgement, the same elegance, the same simplicity, without the smallest affectation, ostentation, profusion, or meanness.' The four grandest rooms including a two-storeyed octagon were occupied by the library, which continued to be expanded throughout the reign to keep pace with the King's bibliomania. By the time of his death in 1820 it comprised 67,000 volumes and had cost £120,000. On George III's accession there had been no royal library because that formed by his predecessors from Henry VIII to George II, and consisting of some 9,000 books, had been given to the newly founded British Museum in 1757 by George II. To replace it, George III immediately began forming a library of his own, replete not just with books but also with maps and medals. The bookcases, folio and medal cabinets for all this were commissioned from the King's favourite cabinet-makers, William Vile and John Bradburn, from 1761 to 1767. Vile supplied cabinets to house 1,600 medals in 1761 and 1762, and for a further 1,385 medals in 1766 and 1767, and this gives an indication of the scale of the King's collecting in the first ten years of his reign. In 1767 Bradburn made map presses costing £260 10s and stands and frames for hanging maps.

The King exercised detailed supervision over the finishing of these rooms and the plans of the cabinet-makers were all submitted to him for his approval, including Bradburn's specification for fitting up the 'Upper Library'. The King himself sometimes provided rough sketches for the hanging of the pictures and so forth to guide the architects, decorators and cabinet-makers, and some of these sketches survive in the Royal Library at Windsor. He was exceedingly meticulous about details, and if some feature of a design displeased him he amended it in his own hand.

The Queen's rooms were far more richly furnished than the King's and were filled with her collections of china, ivories, snuff-boxes, etui, jade, lacquer and pretty *objets de vertu*. The Queen shared many of her husband's tastes, but was less conservative and less averse to lavish effects. Mrs Lybbe Powys, when she visited Buckingham House in 1767, found the Queen's rooms much grander and more elaborately furnished than the King's and filled with 'curiosities from every nation . . . The most capital pictures, the finest Dresden and other china, cabinets of more minute curiosities.' The old two-storeyed saloon of Buckingham House was completely redecorated in a cool grey and gold neo-classical scheme, 'painted in the antique taste' by Cipriani, aided by William Oram, with pilaster strips and gilt oval looking glasses. The white marble chimneypiece, incorporating a clock, was sculpted by John Bacon to Robert Adam's design (and is now at Windsor Castle). The *tout ensemble* was subdued but undoubtedly regal and served as the Queen's throne room when she started holding her 'drawing-rooms' there rather than at St James's, later in the reign. In the centre of the garden front, behind the saloon, was the Red Drawing Room with another drawing room adjoining, both with elegant stucco ceilings embellished with inset paintings by Cipriani, one designed by Robert Adam and one by Sir William Chambers.[6] The room to the south was the Queen's breakfast room, fitted up by Vile in 1763 to incorporate the old lacquer from the central room in the garden front. A visitor in 1802 commented: 'Here are the comforts of a family home, with the grandeur and some of the ornaments of a palace.' These rooms, however, did not make a formal apartment for traditional court functions, and these continued to be held in the old State Rooms at St James's Palace, which were redecorated and much gilded in 1794. The regular functions, until the breakdown of the King's health later in the reign, chiefly comprised levees and drawing-rooms; there was also the occasional court ball and formal receptions of foreign ambassadors. Levees were purely male occasions held by the King and, until his illness, took place regularly on Wednesdays and Fridays (and until 1788 on Mondays when Parliament was sitting) in the morning at St James's Palace. Those admitted mounted the stairs to the King's Guard Chamber and then progressed through the Presence Chamber and Privy Chamber, where there was a choice of direction, with the Little Drawing Room and State Bedchamber to the left, and the Large Drawing Room and Council Chamber to the right. The King would receive formal addresses in the Presence Chamber, such as that presented by the Duke of Norfolk in 1778 on behalf of the Catholics of Britain and Ireland, which resulted in the first degree of Catholic Emancipation. Audiences to his Ministers were granted by the King in the State Bedroom, while the general circle formed in the Drawing Room, where the King walked round saying a few words to everyone and occasionally snubbing somebody of whose public actions he disapproved. Attendance at levees was more or less compulsory for anyone prominent in public and official life. Their purpose was partly ceremonial, in that they comprised presentations of individuals to the monarch, but also still related directly to the business of government, as they were still the occasion when addresses and petitions were presented and offices distributed. They could be exhausting for the King, however, because, if a lot of people attended, he might well be on his feet continuously from 11.00 a.m. to 5.00 p.m. without refreshment.

Drawing-rooms were a weekly event on Thursdays and were attended by both sexes. They too took place in the morning, and were held in the rooms to the right of the Privy Chamber at St James's, but later in the Queen's Rooms at Buckingham House. In the early part of the reign, when the King and Queen were in London, a drawing-room was also held on Sundays after church. But they got fewer as time passed, and by the last years of George III's reign, when the Prince Regent stood in for his father, they were only held 'two or four times a year, and everybody man or woman that assumes the name of gentleman or lady go to it'.

Towards the end of the century the King and Queen spent less time at Buckingham House and more time at Kew, where George III took over his mother's house on her death, and at Windsor, where in 1776 George III gave Queen Charlotte Queen Anne's Lodge to the south of the castle. By the 1790s the King's life was that of a regular commuter, driving at great speed to Windsor on Sunday evening for three nights and then going to London via Kew on Wednesday, staying one night at Buckingham House and then returning

The Queen's House
(Buckingham Palace). The
King's Library.

The Queen's House. The
Queen's Breakfast Room.

to Kew after the drawing-room on Thursday, and so back to Windsor again.

Windsor came to loom more and more prominently in the King's life. The Lodge there was rebuilt between 1778 and 1782 to the design of Sir William Chambers, whose last major work for George III it was, and cost £75,000. The new house was a gloomy castellated pile looking more like a barracks than a royal residence. Horace Walpole described it as being 'plain to the point of meanness', and it was demolished unregretted in 1823 by George IV in order to extend Charles II's Long Walk right up to the Castle. But even in George III's reign the Lodge was displaced by a gradual restoration of the Castle itself and by the Queen's new home at Frogmore, adjoining Windsor Great Park. Frogmore was remodelled for the Queen in 1792 by an architect who came to supersede Chambers as the favourite of the Royal Family, James Wyatt.

Wyatt probably came to the King's attention at the time of the opening of his first major building in London, the Pantheon in Oxford Street, in 1772, and may have been presented to the King by Richard Dalton, the royal librarian, whom Wyatt had met in Venice while on his Grand Tour in the 1760s. Frogmore, a small estate adjoining Windsor, was bought by the King for £8,000 in 1790 and given to the Queen as her personal property to remodel and improve according to her own taste. She first devoted herself to the grounds, which were landscaped with the help of the Revd Mr Alderson, 'a man of great natural taste, but not of the world', and the ornamental lake formed according to the design of the Vice-Chamberlain of her household, Major William Price, brother of Uvedale Price, the Squire of Foxley in Herefordshire and apostle of the Picturesque. Wyatt, as his first work for the Queen, designed some of the ornamental buildings scattered about as focal points in the new layout including a rustic hermit's cottage and a Gothic ruin (still extant), which contained a room decorated with 'Tudor' paintings where the Queen sometimes had breakfast in summer.

The old house at Frogmore was a plain Georgian box, two-storeys high and seven-bays wide. At first the Queen thought of replacing it with a new Gothic 'cottage'. On 13 January 1792, she wrote to Prince Augustus:

Frogmore. Remodelled by James Wyatt for Queen Charlotte.

Wyatt the Architect has made me the prittiest plan imaginable for a Gothic cottage, it consists of four rooms upon a Floor besides the Towers of which there are 4 which will make eight closets alotted for Books, Plants, China and one for the Flower pieces painted by Miss mosert (sic). There will be a colonnade the whole length of the house which will make a sweet retirement in the summer all dressed out with Flowers.[7]

Wyatt made several different designs for Frogmore, and the following year the Queen wrote to the Earl of Ailesbury that he had 'made many pretty tantalizing proposals about my little paradise'. In the event Gothic was abandoned altogether and Frogmore was remodelled, stuccoed and enlarged in the classical style. Wyatt added an extra storey, flanking pavilions with segmental bowed centres, and pairs of characteristic tripartite windows using Doric columns as mullions. This Order was continued to the same scale in the Doric colonnade the length of the west front (now glazed, but originally open), which tied the whole design together and gave the enlarged house an overall architectural consistency and unity. Wyatt also designed the adjoining stables, an attractive composition with two square towers carrying little domed caps and sporting a sundial and a clock.

The interior of Frogmore was arranged to show the Queen's collections to advantage, and though much of Wyatt's elegant neo-classical decoration has disappeared, the appearance of the rooms as they were in Queen Charlotte's lifetime is recorded in Pyne's *Royal Residences*. In the South Pavilion was 'Miss Moser's Room' with the large flower paintings on black grounds by Mary Moser for which she was paid £900. The upholstery in the room was painted to match, with floral motifs on black, and Wyatt designed an unusual chimneypiece of white marble so pure it looks like alabaster, with rams' head consoles and *trompe-l'oeil* frieze carved with fringed drapery, an enchanting conceit. The adjoining library has been dismantled but had cases grained to resemble satinwood, the walls painted brown to tone in with them. Along the top of the cases were black plaster busts of literary figures. The central room in the North Pavilion was the Dining Room, with apsed ends and a blue, red and white colour scheme; on the walls hung a series of Mecklenburg-Strelitz family portraits. Pyne described this exquisite but austere room as being 'fitted up in a style of elegant simplicity, in conformity with the notions of her Majesty'. Other rooms of special interest were the various Japan Rooms fitted with red and black lacquer wall panels, some of it genuine and some of it imitation painted by Princess Elizabeth, George III's talented younger daughter, who spent much of her time at Frogmore with her mother pursuing their shared interests, painting and botanical collections; the Queen even had a printing press there.[8] It is not clear, however, whether the Queen actually lived in the house all the time or merely used to spend the day, going over from Windsor to pursue her own interests there.

The royal family was pleased with Wyatt's work at Frogmore and before long he was entrusted with the transformation of Windsor Castle itself. Work began in 1800 and continued until the King's final illness in 1811 brought the whole project to a halt in a part-finished state, though over £150,000 had been spent. George III's interest in Windsor in middle age was prompted by his political outlook and the impact on it of national circumstances. He was a 'natural conservative' and instinctively revered ancient institutions like the Church and the Monarchy. Such views had made him unpopular at the beginning of the reign in the face of Wilkes and Liberty and the loss of the American colonies, but the French Revolution changed all that. The overthrow of the traditional

Frogmore. The Dining
Room. The portraits are of
the Mecklenburg-Strelitz
family.

Frogmore. The Library.

Windsor. The Tomb House made by George III.

Windsor Castle. The King's Audience Chamber as redecorated in 1786 by George III with historical canvases of Edward III and the Black Prince.

structure of society across the channel provoked a strong feeling of revulsion in England and fuelled the High Tory reaction of Burke and Pitt, suddenly making the King and all he symbolized extremely popular as the embodiment of English tradition. At the same time attitudes towards the Middle Ages changed, as people wished to emphasize traditional values and the continuity of English institutions. Thus Windsor, the ancient seat of the monarchy, came to have a special significance. George III, who in his youth had been a dyed-in-the-wool Palladian, found himself moved by Windsor's associational qualities and suddenly became an enthusiastic convert to Gothic. He wrote to the Duchess of Wurtemburg: 'I never thought I should have adopted Gothic instead of Grecian Architecture, but the bad taste of the last fifty years has so entirely corrupted the professors of the latter, I have taken to the former from thinking

Wyatt perfect in that style.' The King had already restored St George's Chapel in the 1780s and 1790s under the direction of Henry Emlyn, and had made some alterations to the state rooms with the help of John Yenn, an architect-pupil of Sir William Chambers, and Benjamin West, the American-born artist, who made a series of large historical paintings of subjects in the life of Edward III. The King's Audience Chamber was modernized in 1786, when a new marble chimneypiece was inserted and the walls hung with Garter-blue velvet trimmed with floral needlework borders designed by Mary Moser and worked by Mrs Pawley's school of needlework. The canopy of state over the new throne had matching needlework and was supported by painted pilasters designed by Benjamin West and executed by Biagio Rebecca.

These works formed the overture to Wyatt's more sweeping transformation of the state apartments into a Gothic palace. Hugh May's windows were replaced with pointed Gothic ones (discernible from Wyatville's by the use of white Portland stone tracery), a double-decker cloister was built round the Horn Court on the model of Wilton, and a new grand entrance formed from the quadrangle, which was lowered two feet by excavating the surface. Inside the north block a suite of private apartments was formed for George III on the ground floor, and there he was confined during the melancholy years of his illness, the sentries pacing the terrace outside saluting when they saw his wild unshaven face staring blankly out of the window. Wyatt also designed a new Grand Staircase on the site of the old King's Stair, with a plaster Gothic vault by Bernasconi (still *in situ*) and a balustrade of bronzed ironwork with polished brass ornament. The Charles II state apartments on the first floor were considerably altered, some of them enlarged, but keeping to their existing style. The new ceilings painted by Francis Rigaud and Matthew Cotes Wyatt were in a baroque manner similar to Verrio's. The Grinling Gibbons carvings were also repaired by Edward Wyatt, as was the old furniture. Some of the rooms were hung with silk brocade, and new chandeliers installed. Unfortunately this sympathetic conservationist approach to the Charles II apartments did not extend into the next reign, and Wyatville destroyed all except three of the old ensembles and replaced the painted ceilings with commonplace designs of gilded stucco.

As well as the work to the state apartments, George III also restored the Tomb House east of St George's Chapel in the Lower Ward. He formed a large new burial vault underneath and fitted up the chapel interior with a plaster Gothic vault and paintings by Matthew Cotes Wyatt to form a chapterhouse for the Order of the Garter.[9] George III's conservative, historicist, even reverential approach to Windsor is revealed in Pyne's remarks about the bed in the King's State Bedroom: 'Queen Anne's bed which being valued by his present Majesty is preserved with care, having a crimson curtain to draw over it, and it is guarded from the rude approach of idle curiosity by a screen in front.' As part of the mystique of Windsor, the King designed a special Windsor uniform to be worn by gentlemen when at court in the castle; it was of blue cloth with red and gold facings, and is still worn at dinner at Windsor today. In April 1805 he revived the ceremony of installation of Knights of the Garter, for which event St George's Hall was fitted with an organ and music gallery, and its wallpaintings were cleaned and restored. Though the King was increasingly stirred by the historic and chivalric associations of Windsor, Queen Charlotte was far less enthusiastic and wrote to a friend in 1804: 'We are now returned to our new habitation in the castle. Not to shock you . . . with my opinion on this subject

I will briefly tell you that I have changed from a very comfortable and warm habitation to the coldest house, rooms and passages that ever existed.'

The King loved playing the role of country squire – 'Farmer George' – at Windsor, and on the death of the Duke of Cumberland in 1790 he took over the direct management of Windsor Great Park. He laid out there two large farms with the advice of Nathaniel Kent, a leading agricultural theorist of the period. Each farm was managed according to a different pattern of cultivation: the Norfolk Farm of a thousand acres of light soil according to a five-year rotation, and the Flemish Farm of four hundred acres of heavier, loamy soil according to the Flemish four-year rotation. It is wholly characteristic of George III's approach to the royal houses and estates that he should have occupied himself in laying out two model farms in Windsor Great Park, rather than indulging in elaborate landscaping and gardening projects. He took a very close personal interest in the development of these two farms and even designed some of the buildings himself, including a little Palladian cottage for his swineherd. He also wrote various pieces on farming-method, drawing on his experience at the Windsor farms, which he submitted to the Board of Agriculture under the *nom de plume* of his shepherd, Ralph Robinson. At Frogmore he built a dairy adjoining the cowsheds, which was a pretty little octagonal structure with a fountain in the middle of the milk room where the butter, milk and cream were prepared for the royal table. He liked to visit his farms and dairy every morning when he was in residence at Windsor, and he was a well-known local figure, walking unattended through the park, which in the eighteenth century as now was freely open to the public.[10]

Charles Knight, the son of a local bookseller, recalled:

The park was a glory for cricket and kite-flying. The King would stand alone to see the boys at cricket. He was a quiet good-humoured gentleman in a long blue coat; and many a time had he bidden us good morning when we were hunting for mushrooms in the early

Kew Palace. Designed and built by James Wyatt for George III but demolished in 1827. It was nicknamed 'The Bastille' by radical critics.

dew and he was returning from his dairy to his eight o'clock breakfast. Everyone knew that most respectable and amicable of country squires, and His Majesty knew everyone.[11]

George III had never given up his ambition of erecting a new palace at Kew (Richmond), and the reconstruction of Windsor was not intended as a substitute for that. In 1800 he once more revived the project for building a royal palace overlooking the Thames in the Old Deer Park. The commission was awarded to James Wyatt, and the Palladian style of Chambers's unexecuted schemes now gave way to Gothic. The new palace was to be a symmetrical castellated pile, and like the restoration of Windsor was intended as an architectural demonstration of the authority and tradition of the English Crown. As such it was much criticized by the radicals, who nicknamed it the 'Bastille'. George Dance complained to John Soane that 'the rascally Democrats have lately made it their stalking horse'. Other critics saw its castellated silhouette as a Spenserian fantasy, or even as a symptom of the King's madness. It was built to a symmetrical plan, with a large square main block, each front of which was evenly punctuated by four cylindrical towers. In the centre was a large imperial plan staircase rising under a high, square keep-like tower, and ranged on either side of this were two parallel series of state apartments. In front of the main block was an enclosed courtyard with rounded corners, entered through an arched gatehouse on axis with the main entrance. This forecourt was flanked on either hand by subsidiary stable and office wings. By 1811, when the King's final illness brought work to a halt, over £500,000 had been spent and the brick shell had been completed, though the interiors still remained to be fitted up. In fact Kew never was finished, for George IV did not like it, and the whole structure was demolished in 1827. All that remains is one cast-iron traceried window built into a potting shed in Kew Gardens. Like Charles II's Winchester Palace, George III's Kew is one of the tragic abortive episodes in English architecture, a huge, expensive structure never finished, soon demolished, and now almost forgotten.[12]

Despite its incomplete state and short existence, Kew Palace made an impact on contemporary architectural development. Its plan was the model for James Wyatt's final Gothic masterpiece, Ashridge in Hertfordshire, and it was also the inspiration for Smirke's two influential castle-houses – Lowther Castle in Westmorland and Eastnor Castle in Herefordshire. In its construction, too, George III's Kew Palace broke new ground. It was one of the earliest examples in English architecture of fireproof construction, all the internal supports being of cast-iron, as were all the Gothic traceried window casements. James Wyatt's fireproof construction at Kew was probably based on his brother Samuel's patent for cast-iron construction evolved after the burning of the Albion Mill at Blackfriars, and the immediate future of fireproof construction in England was to be in industrial and warehouse buildings rather than in domestic architecture. It is sad that so spectacular and original a building should have survived such a short time and been no more than a very costly folly. In the last resort George III did not complete any of his palace projects because he only spent what he had, rather than what he had not. This, however, was not a constraint which his son ever recognized.

IX

GEORGE IV

George IV was the only major patron of the arts produced by the Hanoverian dynasty, and it is almost entirely due to him that the English monarchy today has any palaces worthy of the name. Reacting against the simple domesticity of his father's life, he set about providing himself with settings worthy of the 'monarch of the richest and most powerful nation in the world'. At Windsor he created a Romantic feudal pile grander than anything of the kind in existence; at Buckingham Palace he contrived an elegant, Francophile royal residence which goes some way towards filling the gap caused by the loss of Westminster and Whitehall; and at Brighton he erected one of the last as well as one of the most extravagant and certainly the most exotic of those casinos or pavilions which had been such a delightful feature of eighteenth-century royal building in Europe. In retrospect, George IV's building activity can be seen to have formed three main phases of increasing magnificence, reflecting his political position. When young, he was satisfied with elegant Louis XVI rooms of exquisite restraint as a civilized setting for a comparatively carefree existence at Carlton House (Phase I) and Brighton Pavilion (Phase I). On becoming Regent in middle age, he found that he needed grander settings for a more formal court life and for official business – extra state rooms as well as rooms for audiences and council meetings – and this brought about an extensive remodelling of Carlton House and the enlargement and reconstruction of Brighton Pavilion, as well as the creation of a commodious country house, the Royal Lodge in Windsor Great Park. Finally, on succeeding to the throne at a time of national triumph, he envisaged a completely new scale of existence with Buckingham Palace and Windsor Castle reconstructed at enormous cost to form appropriate state palaces.

In his personal taste George IV was strongly Francophile, and in the course of his life he brought together the finest collection of French decorative art ever assembled outside France. This taste was partly the result of his early education and was partly due to the influence of his friends. Both predisposed him to favour French culture. He spoke the language perfectly, and his correspondence with his mother, for instance, was conducted in French. His reading, too, as testified by his purchases of books, included many literary, historical and military works from France. When he came of age in 1783 and was given his own independent establishment, he immediately identified himself with the Whig opposition, partly in filial reaction against his father's Toryism. The

Whigs, especially their leaders – Fox and Sheridan, the Spencers, the Cavendishes and the Russells – were by inclination and policy strongly Francophile, and this helped to increase the Prince's own predilection for French things. Henry Holland was the leading Whig architect, and so he became the Prince's architect. Holland's refined anglicized version of *le style Louis XVI* was the perfect expression of the Prince's youthful taste.

The Prince also had many French friends, including the Duc d'Orleans (Philippe Egalité), whose wife's fortune made him one of the richest men in France and whose splendid portrait by Reynolds hung at Carlton House; though temporarily removed at the time of the French Revolution, it was replaced following the restoration of the French monarchy in 1815. The Prince's revulsion from France brought about by the excesses of the Revolution was shortlived, but it had important side-effects on his architectural patronage. It was one of the reasons for his switch from French decoration to oriental at Brighton Pavilion. In 1797 *The Times* reported with approval that the Prince intended to dismiss all Frenchmen from his service and expressed the hope that every nobleman would follow his example. In fact the Prince did not carry out this threat, and it was with a certain irony that he complained to Lady Bessborough that 'there was such a cry against French things etc., that he was afraid of his furniture being accus'd of Jacobinism'.[1]

This hiatus marked a change in the character of George IV's Francophilia. While in early life he had identified himself with the more progressive elements in contemporary French life, in later years it was to the *Grand Siècle* that he looked back with nostalgia, and he modelled himself and his rooms on Louis XIV and Louis XV. The so-called '*Louis Quatorze*' style with its boulle, rococo and lashings of gilt replaced the simpler elegance of Henry Holland, Pernotin and Jacob.

George IV had great sense of style and feeling for occasion. When he opened Parliament in state it was with an almost theatrical flair, while his coronation, in which all the participants wore specially designed 'Tudor' dress, was the grandest in post-Reformation English history. In creating a setting for his court, it was to Versailles and the Tuilleries that he looked for inspiration. His purchase of French works of art was partly an attempt to recreate for his own receptions an ambiance similar to that which had provided the background to the ritual of the old court of France. In his youth he had bought contemporary French furniture from Paris through fashionable dealers like Dominique Daguerre, but with the systematic dispersal of the contents of the French royal palaces by the revolutionaries, he was able to secure many earlier masterpieces of French eighteenth-century furniture as well as the Dutch cabinet paintings which were their fashionable accompaniment. For these later purchases he relied heavily on members of his household acting as his agents, including Louis Weltje, his cook, and François Benois, his confectioner. At a higher social level, several courtiers and members of the 'Carlton House set' were keenly interested in art and architecture and acted as advisers to the King on matters of taste. Chief of these was Sir Charles Long, later Lord Farnborough, the *éminence grise* behind much of George IV's activity as a connoisseur of art and patron of architecture. Long, for example, vetted many of the King's more important purchases of works of art, travelling to Paris on occasion for this purpose, and was directly responsible for supervising the schemes of restoration and decoration adopted at St James's Palace, Windsor Castle and Buckingham Palace in the 1820s.

The Prince first had the opportunity to express his own taste in 1783, when he

Old Carlton House from Pall Mall, showing the jumble of buildings which Henry Holland transformed into a unified palace for George IV.

was given Carlton House in Pall Mall as his official residence and was voted £60,000 by Parliament for its rehabilitation. The house had a good site overlooking St James's Park to the south, but though it had been a royal residence since 1732, it left a great deal to be desired architecturally, and looked more like an irregular group of independent buildings than a single house. It was, moreover, considered to be old-fashioned, and had been unoccupied for ten years. When bought by Frederick, Prince of Wales, in 1732 from the Dowager Countess of Burlington, it comprised a seventeenth-century house recently remodelled by Henry Flitcroft.[2] Frederick had landscaped the garden overlooking St James's Park to the design of William Kent, and in 1762 his widow, George III's mother, had enlarged the house to form her dower house by taking over Bubb Doddington's house next door. For a time she had toyed with the idea of disguising the irregular Pall Mall front (really the back) by erecting an elegant neo-classical screen-wall designed by Robert Adam, but nothing came of that.[3] Following her death the house had been left empty.

When the Prince took over the house, Sir William Chambers, the Surveyor-General, supervised some necessary repairs at a cost of £6,000, but the Prince did not want Chambers, who in his eyes was too much George III's man, and after employing Guillame Gaubert, a French cook-turned-decorator, to do some work, he appointed Henry Holland as his own architect to transform the

Carlton House. The entrance front with Corinthian portico designed by Henry Holland.

unpromising old house into a palace comparable in quality if not in scale with any in Europe. Holland's work was done in stages over two decades, the improvement of the garden front with its central canted bay and the creation of the south front state rooms with private rooms beneath for the Prince's own occupation being executed first. By 1785 enough had been done to send Horace Walpole into raptures:

> I have been two days in town to meet Mr Conway and Lady Aylesbury. We went to see the Prince's new Palace in Pall Mall; and were charmed. It will be the most perfect in Europe.
> There is an August simplicity that astonished one. You cannot call it magnificent; it is the taste and propriety that strike. Every ornament is at a proper distance, and not one too large, but all delicate and new; and, though probably borrowed from the Hôtel de Condé and other new Palaces, not one that is not rather classic than French . . . there are three most spacious apartments, all looking over the lovely garden; a terreno, the state apartment and an attic.
> The portico, vestibule, hall and staircase will be superb, and to my taste, full of perspectives; the jewel of all is a small musicroom, that opens into a green recess and winding walk of the garden . . .[4]

In 1785, however, work was seriously interrupted by the first of the recurrent financial crises which were to bedevil all George IV's architectural projects. He was totally irresponsible in money matters. He approved his architects' schemes, and with great enthusiasm commissioned new projects, without any thought for where the money was coming from to pay for them. By 1785 he had accumulated

Carlton House. The
garden front.

Below: Carlton House,
Henry Holland's Plan
for the Principal Floor,
circa 1790

 1 *Forecourt*
 2 *Kitchen Wing*
 3 *Portico*
 4 *Hall*
 5 *Octagon*
 6 *Staircase*
 7 *Ante Chambers*
 8 *Grand Eating Room*
 9 *Music Room*
10 *Great Drawing Room*
11 *Throne Room*
12 *Her Royal Highness's
   Private Drawing Room*
13 *Salon*
14 *Bed Chamber*
15 *Library*

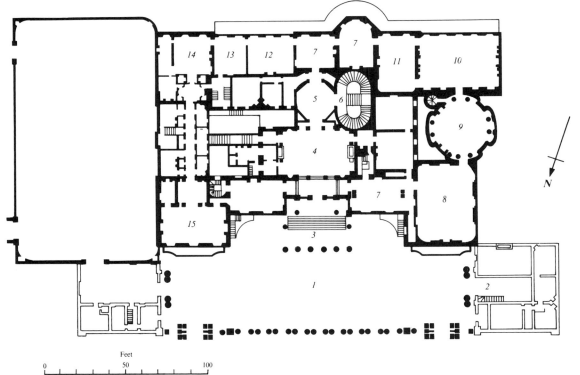

Feet

0   50   100

vertiginous debts. Unpaid bills amounted to £250,000. The Prince sold his racehorses for £7,000. Work at Carlton House was stopped, and he retired to Brighton for his health and to economize by leading the simple life with Mrs Fitzherbert, a beautiful Catholic widow whom he had secretly married. There he indulged in the new fashion for sea bathing which he hoped would cure the ugly swelling of the glands in his neck (which was the chief reason for the high stocks, collars and cravats which he affected and which he made the fashion).

Brighton had begun to develop as a resort in the 1760s and 70s, following the discovery by Dr Richard Russell of Lewes that sea bathing had a beneficial effect on swollen glands, upon which subject he wrote a bestselling treatise, *De Tabe Glandulari*, the English translation of which ran into several editions with the result that people

Rushed coastward to be cur'd like tongues
By dipping into brine.

In 1771 the Prince's uncle, the Duke of Cumberland, had bought himself a house at what was then still called Brighthelmstone, and when he came of age the Prince stayed there several times, attracted by the Duke's slightly disreputable reputation and by the entertainments provided – women, dances, races, theatre and sea bathing. In 1784 the Prince had rented Grove House on the Steine, through the mediation of Weltje, and the following year Weltje had taken a three-year lease of a farmhouse belonging to Thomas Read Kemp, which lay to the south of Grove House. The lease gave the opportunity of buying the house, provided it was rebuilt. This option was exercised by Weltje in 1787, and he subsequently devised the property to the Prince, whose financial straits had by that time been eased by a Parliamentary grant of £161,000 towards payment of his debts, together with an extra £60,000 for the completion of Carlton House, provided he married a German princess of his father's choice, a condition which had disastrous consequences.[5]

Holland produced a revised estimate of £49,700 in May 1787 for completing the north front of Carlton House, for which the designs had already been 'made and approved' and which Horace Walpole had seen two years previously, before the crisis in the Prince's finances. Holland contrived out of the existing congeries of buildings a symmetrical two-storeyed front faced in Portland stone and dignified by a central hexastyle Corinthian portico wide enough for carriages to drive under like a porte-cochère, which was something of an innovation in English architecture. Behind the portico was a dramatic sequence of large entrance hall, two-storeyed central octagonal tribune and an oval imperial plan staircase going up to the 'attic' floor and down to the 'terreno', the garden front being one storey lower than the street front. The forecourt to Pall Mall was enclosed and dignified by an Ionic screen of Parisian derivation. Work was finished by 1789, and the Prince was able to hold his first levee in the completed Carlton House in 1790.[6]

No proper record survives of the interior of Carlton House as created by Henry Holland. Pyne's famous views of the house in 1819 show the rooms after extensive remodelling by other hands, and only the scrappiest sketches and a few plans survive of Holland's own designs. With their help, however, it is possible to work out something of the appearance of the house in its earliest and finest state. The hall, octagon and staircase survived relatively unchanged throughout, while the circular Music Room, Great Drawing Room and Eating Room added at the west end of the house retained some of Holland's decoration

Opposite: Carlton House. The oval main staircase designed by Henry Holland.

Carlton House. Designs by
Edward Wyatt for
decorative panels in the
Scagliola Room on the
'Terreno'.

to the end. Perhaps Holland's finest achievement was to contrive a coherent
plan out of the irregular jumble of old buildings on the cramped site, even
though the central axes of the two fronts did not meet. The Entrance Hall was
an extremely handsome neo-classical room with a coffered segmental ceiling,
statues in niches and at either end as well as at the centre of the long walls, and
Ionic screens of yellow Sienna scagliola columns (made by Bartoli) supporting
beams with bronzed urns and griffins inspired by the Aldobrandini relief in
Rome, which had been sketched for Holland by his pupil C. H. Tatham. Beyond
the hall in the centre of the house was the octagonal vestibule open to the upper
gallery through an oculus, giving glimpses of the elaborate fan-patterned stucco
ceiling above. An arch to the right gave access to the staircase, its French
patterned balustrade painted blue and gold. The views from the hall through
the octagon to the staircase and upper landings provided the chief spatial
excitement of Carlton House. The dramatic effect was enhanced by the top-
lighting of the staircase and octagon through skylights filled with pretty painted
glass copied from Raphael's *grotteschi* in the Vatican loggia. The three state
rooms of which aspects of Holland's decoration are recorded were the Great
Drawing Room (later Throne Room), the Music Room, and the Eating Room
(later Crimson Drawing Room). The Eating Room had a stuccoed ceiling of
sparsely arranged neo-classical motifs reminiscent of the Canaletto Room at

Woburn Abbey. The Great Drawing Room had a stuccoed ceiling embellished with painted Raphaelesque *grotteschi*, possibly the 'antique grotesque' work for which Biagio Rebecca was paid £110 in 1794. The circular Music Room between the two other apartments was an Ionic rotunda of 'Porfido Rosso' (porphyry) scagliola columns by Bartoli, with tented alcoves flanked by Frenchy pilaster strips and panels painted by one of the Prince's French decorators – Louis Delabrière (who had worked for the Comte d'Artois at Bagatelle) or T. H. Pernotin – and a shallow domed ceiling painted to resemble a sky. These rooms were furnished with Louis XVI furniture mainly imported through Dominique Daguerre in 1787.

While it is possible, therefore, to gain some idea of Holland's state rooms at Carlton House as they were in their pristine state, fresh, elegant, restrained and beautifully balanced, next to nothing is known about the suite of rooms beneath on the 'terreno'. One drawing room had walls lined with scagliola, which must have created a somewhat Russian effect, but only the appearance of the Salon Chinois, designed in June 1789, is recorded.[7] The furniture provided for this room also still survives in the royal collection. It comprises two ormolu-mounted side-tables, a marble chimneypiece with ormolu mounts *en suite*, and a set of

Carlton House. The entrance hall designed by Henry Holland.

gilt chairs with Buddhas on top, covered in yellow satin of dragon pattern to match the curtains. Holland's inspiration for the decoration of this charming but shortlived room was Sir William Chambers's *Designs for Chinese Buildings*, published in 1757. There had been some controversy as to whether this furniture, so strongly reminiscent of Weisweiler, was of English or French manufacture. W. H. Pyne in 1819, however, when the furniture had been moved upstairs to the Rose Satin Drawing Room, went out of his way to say that it was mainly English.[8]

While work at Carlton House was drawing to a successful conclusion, Holland had in 1787 produced plans for a speedy remodelling and enlargement of the Prince's little house at Brighton in an equally Francophile but less opulent taste. Over £24,454 18s 2d was spent on a new domed circular centre and on duplicating the old house to create a symmetrical enfilade of rooms – library, eating room, and circular saloon in the new part, and an ante-room and breakfast room in the old. A wide corridor or gallery was added at the rear to provide comfortable access to the main rooms. The whole of the exterior was faced in 'Hampshire weather tiles' to simulate stone, rather like Holland's contemporary refacing of Althorp, which still survives. The principal feature of the façade was the domed centrepiece encircled with columns, derived from Rousseau's *Hôtel de Salm* in Paris (1782–6), and the conscious Frenchness of the design was emphasized by the name of the house: it was the Prince's Marine Pavilion, echoing the name of the Comte d'Artois's *pavillon* at Bagatelle.

The decoration of the rooms at Brighton as first completed by Holland is known only from written descriptions and a Rowlandson drawing of the saloon. They were simpler and more relaxed than Carlton House, but in their lower key just as French. The circular saloon had painted pilaster strips by Biagio Rebecca. The library was 'fitted up in the French style' with a brilliant yellow paper. The eating room was yellow too, but with maroon trim and a ceiling of sky blue.

Carlton House. The Circular Room, largely as designed by Henry Holland with porphyry scagliola columns.

The corridor was 'French blue', while the staircase walls were green with a grey and white ceiling.

Both Carlton House and Brighton remained as created by Holland for about ten years, but by the turn of the century the Prince, always restless in architectural matters, was itching to change everything. Holland withdrew from royal patronage in 1802, and so the Prince turned to James Wyatt, who had succeeded Chambers as Royal Surveyor-General, to supervise the refurbishment of the state rooms at Carlton House from 1804 onwards. At first this was intended to be no more than whitewashing and regilding, but like all the Prince's schemes it rapidly got out of hand and resulted in a drastic remodelling of all the state rooms on the main floor and the creation of a new series of semi-state rooms on the 'terreno'. The Prince was egged on in this project by Walsh Porter, one of those eccentric dandies like Brummel or Skeffington who formed a characteristic part of the 'Carlton House set' and lived lives of fashionable extravagance on credit, life insurance, art dealing and similar slightly shady financial legerdemain. Porter was a self-styled connoisseur who wrote a comic opera but, according to Sir Francis Bourgeois, 'had not the least real knowledge of pictures'. Farington noted in 1806 that 'Although Carlton House as finished by Holland was in a complete and new state (the Prince) has ordered the whole to be done again under the direction of Walsh Porter who has destroyed all that Holland has done and is substituting a finishing in a most expensive and motley taste'.[9] Porter at this stage acted as the Prince's decorative consultant, and introduced to him the young Thomas Hopper, who designed a fantastic iron and glass Gothic conservatory in 1807, a masterpiece of intricate casting which led out of the ground-floor rooms to the west.

James Wyatt also brought in under his wing a number of relations: his son Matthew Cotes Wyatt to do decorative painting, his nephews Lewis as labourer in trust and Jeffry as holder of the carpentry contract, and his cousin Edward as carver and gilder. Following James Wyatt's death in 1813, John Nash succeeded him in the Prince's service and made further alterations and embellishments. It is chiefly the work of this variegated team which is shown in Pyne's views. Holland's rooms were overladen with outrageously extravagant, pleated and fringed drapery, huge looking glasses, carvings encrusted with gilt, and chandeliers as big as fountains. The reticent Louis XVI furniture was displaced by the finest treasures of the French royal collections and heavy gilded seat furniture of antique derivation, provided by Morel and Hughes or Tatham & Co., while the walls were hung two or three deep in excellent Dutch pictures and the floors covered with wall to wall carpeting of blue velvet, semé with gold fleurs-de-lis. The over-heated atmosphere heavy with perfumes is only hinted at by the ormolu-mounted incense burners and cassolettes. Everywhere Holland's light, elegant colours gave way to the stronger, classically inspired colours of the early nineteenth century. The entrance hall, for instance, was livened up by marbling the dado 'verde antico', painting the walls granite green, and bronzing all the capitals and mouldings.

These alterations were not just a whim of taste on the Prince's part, but were partly a response to his becoming Regent on the illness of his father. Carlton House was no longer just the residence of the heir to the throne, but the seat of the court and the palace from which state business had to be conducted: foreign ambassadors accredited, privy council meetings convened, ministers received in audience. This made necessary a larger throne room and audience chamber. The old Throne Room was converted into an ante-room and embellished with gilt trophies by Edward Wyatt, including trophies over the doors of the four Orders of Chivalry: the Garter, the Bath, the Thistle, and St Patrick, while Henry Holland's Great Drawing Room beyond was converted into a new Throne Room and suitably enriched with gilded Corinthian pilasters and red velvet drapery. The ante-rooms and drawing rooms along the south front were also upgraded in a consistent style and provided with carved and gilded doors by Edward Wyatt, their panels carved with trophies of Architecture, Commerce, Painting, Navigation, etc. At the east end of the enfilade, the rooms originally intended for the Queen's occupation (she and George IV spent only one night together) were transformed into the two Blue Velvet Rooms to serve as the Prince's private audience chambers, and redecorated with blue velvet panels framed in peach-coloured borders with gilt margins. These served as a background to first-rate paintings including Rembrandt's great double portrait of a ship builder and his wife. Edward Wyatt provided more carved and gilt doors, while the ceilings were painted like a sky and the coves with panels depicting British naval and military triumphs. These alterations on the piano nobile displaced the dining rooms and libraries to the 'terreno' below. The lower rooms were converted by Nash, James Wyatt and Hopper to provide an additional sequence of semi-state rooms which made up for their low proportions by over-rich decoration. The Corinthian Room, for instance, was among the most gilded ensembles ever contrived in England. Some of these lower rooms were Gothic, including the two libraries and Nash's Gothic Dining Room, a peculiar design with a fretted and bracketed ceiling where all the carving and gilding was carried out by Edward Wyatt, who performed the same task in George IV's palaces as Verberckt did in Louis XV's.[10]

The transformation of Brighton Pavilion in the same years was even more spectacular than that of Carlton House. The Prince's interest in chinoiserie had been stimulated by a gift of some oriental wallpaper in 1801, and he used it to redecorate the gallery at the Pavilion in the Chinese taste. Gradually the Chinese influence spread throughout the whole building, drawing strength from the Prince's shortlived hostility to France, which caused him to look East to the British Empire for inspiration, though it was also partly influenced by his mother's interest in Eastern things. She, for instance, had rooms decorated with lacquer at Frogmore and Buckingham House, an Indian Room furnished with a set of ivory chairs given her by Warren Hastings, and most exciting of all, Tipoo Sahib's tent captured from Seringapatam set up on the lawn at Frogmore. So pleased was she by the exotic transformation of Brighton, that she gave her son £50,000 towards the cost out of her privy purse.[11]

Henry Holland produced a scheme for remodelling the outside of the Pavilion *à la chinois* in 1802, but nothing came of this, though two new rooms were added at either end to P. F. Robinson's design.[12] But in 1804–8 a magnificent domed stable block with riding school was built to the design of William Porden in 'Saracenic taste' at a cost of £54,000 and on a scale to overshadow completely the existing house. This set a new scale for future developments. Humphrey Repton, who had advised on the gardens at Carlton House, was summoned to Brighton in 1806 to make plans for remodelling the Pavilion. He was impressed by Porden's work, which he described as 'a stupendous and magnificent building which by its lightness, its elegance, its boldness of construction and symmetry of its proportions, does credit both to the genius of the artist and the good taste of his royal employer. Although the outline of the dome resembles rather a Turkish mosque than the buildings of Hindustan, yet its general character is

Carlton House. Carved and
gilt door by Edward Wyatt
from the Blue Velvet
Room. (Now at Windsor
Castle.)

Carlton House in 1825

1 *Forecourt*
2 *Crimson Drawing
   Room*
3 *Ante Room*
4 *Kitchen*
5 *Circular Room*
6 *Hall*
7 *Throne Room*
8 *Old Throne Room*
9 *Rose Drawing Room*
10 *Ante Room*
11 *Octagon*
12 *Blue Velvet Room*
13 *Dining Room*
14 *Bow Room*
15 *Ante Room*
16 *Library*
17 *Corinthian Room*
18 *Gothic Dining Room*
19 *Conservatory*

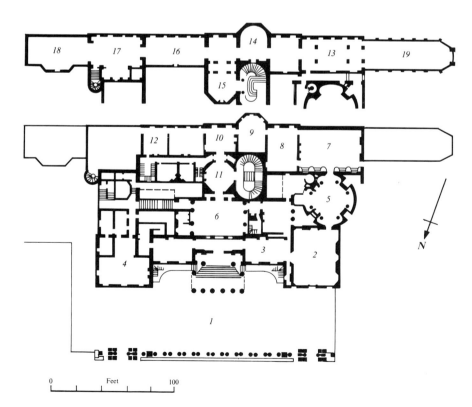

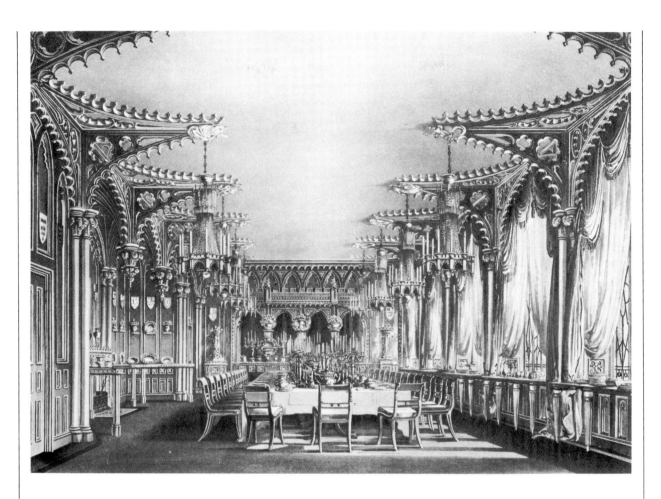

Carlton House. The Gothic Dining Room designed by John Nash with carving and gilding by Edward Wyatt.

distinct from either Grecian or Gothic and must both please and surprise everyone not bigoted to the favour of either.'[13] Repton took this as the cue for his own proposals, which were in the 'Hindustan' manner and drew heavily for their details on the Indian views of William Daniell and William Hodges. Repton's proposals were bound in a handsome folio volume and presented to the Prince, who expressed himself delighted: 'Mr Repton I consider the whole of this work as perfect, and will have every part of it carried into immediate execution, not a tittle shall be altered – even you yourself shall not attempt any improvement.'[14]

The Prince's finances, however, were not up to it, and ten years were to pass before the Indian transformation of the Pavilion took place and then the job, to Repton's bitter disappointment, was entrusted to his erstwhile partner John Nash, who carried out the work in stages – the entrance hall and gallery in 1815, the kitchen in 1816, the new end wings in 1817, the old centre remodelled in 1818 and the private apartments in 1819. The result is one of the best-known Picturesque buildings in England, with its fantastic onion-shaped domes and conical roofs forming the 'apotheosis of the tent', its fretted loggias, its minarets and Saracenic arches. The rooms in the old centre were redecorated in richer Indian-Chinese to make them harmonize with the two large new state rooms at either end, which formed the major feature of the building. Each was 60 feet by 40 feet and rose the full height of the building, one the Music Room and the

Opposite: Carlton House. The cast iron Gothic conservatory designed by Thomas Hopper in 1807.

other the Dining Room. Both were lavishly decorated with wall paintings influenced by lacquer and silk screens and embellished with all the bamboo and dragons imaginable. The climax of each was a domed ceiling carried on convex coving, breaking away from all established canons of Georgian architectural taste, and supporting gigantic chandeliers of fantastic appearance. Both rooms are almost too grand for their setting, a feature commented on by contemporaries: 'The Music-Room is most splendid, but I think the other handsomer. they are both too handsome for Brighton, and in an excessive degree too fine for the extent of his Royal Highness's premises. It is a great pity that the whole of the suite of rooms was not solidly built in or near London.'[15]

The Prince himself came to feel the constriction and lack of privacy of Brighton, and after he ascended the throne he visited it less and less, finally leaving in 1827 never to return. What had begun as a charming retreat from the responsibilities and constraints of the capital had itself become something of a nightmare, as the new town grew up all round the Pavilion and the King found himself surrounded by an inquisitive and not always respectful populace. It is best to remember the earlier years at Brighton, the period of Mrs Fitzherbert's first and second ascendancies, when all was easy comfort and happy freedom. Lady Bessborough recorded a typical day in 1805:

Brighton Pavilion. The stables and riding school by William Porden in 'Saracenic taste'.

20. The Crimson Drawing Room, Queen's House. Aquatint from W. H. Pyne Royal Residences *(1819).*

21. The Blue Velvet Room, Carlton House. Aquatint from W. H. Pyne Royal Residences *(1819).*

22. OPPOSITE: *The Dining Room, Brighton Pavilion.*

23. RIGHT: *Garden front, Buckingham Palace.*

24. BELOW: *The Ball Room, Buckingham Palace. Watercolour by Croft.*

*25. The Royal Dairy,
Frogmore.*

His way of living is pleasant enough, especially if one might chuse one's society. In the Morning he gives you horses, Carriages etc., to go where you please with you; he comes and sits *rather too long*, but only on a visit. Everybody meets at dinner, which, par parenthèse, is excellent, with the addition of a few invitations in the evening. Three large rooms, very comfortable, are lit up; whist, backgammon, Chess, tracc Madame – every sort of game you can think of in two of them, and Musick in the third. His band is beautiful. He has Viotti and a Lady who sings and plays very well. A few people have the entrée and a few more are invited.[16]

Some visitors grumbled that the Pavilion was *too* comfortable, the rooms too overheated, too much light, too much cherry brandy, and too much rich food. Certainly after Nash's reconstruction it was one of the most comfortable houses in Europe. The kitchen, for instance, was the perfection of modern gadgetry, filled with all sorts of ovens and spits, running hot and cold water and piped steam, even vapour baths. It was also one of the first houses in the world to have gas lighting, with chandeliers installed for burning gas as early as 1818.

Fond though he was of Brighton, the Prince and his circle did not consider it suitable as the only country residence for the Regent of the English throne. He needed as well a commodious retreat somewhere nearer London, and also near Windsor Castle, where the old King was detained. Lower Lodge in the Great

Brighton Pavilion as made Indian by John Nash between 1815 and 1819.

Park, where Thomas Sandby the watercolourist had once lived, was chosen, and an estimate approved by the Treasury for its enlargement. Nash produced designs for the alterations. The old cottage was to be transformed into the Royal Lodge, stuccoed and thatched outside and rearranged inside, a conservatory and trellised verandahs added, all at a cost of £17,000. The result was an extremely pretty *cottage orné*. Nash was at pains to make it look as small as possible, and the surrounding plantations were carefully arranged so that not too much of the building would be visible in any one view, though the game was given away by the large array of chimney-stacks on the skyline. The entrance front with two gables was becomingly modest, though the long front round the corner was more impressive with its 'bonneted dormers', rustic verandah, and cast-iron conservatory and 'trellised temple' concealing the service quarters. As Lord Brougham remarked, 'though called a cottage because it happened to be thatched, it was still a very comfortable residence.'[17]

The death of his father and George IV's accession to the throne completely altered the scale of his architectural thinking. Carlton House, Brighton Pavilion and Royal Lodge had been good enough for the Prince of Wales, even the Prince Regent, but for the King of the United Kingdom of Great Britain and Ireland establishments of an altogether grander type were required: a metropolitan state palace on a European scale and a country seat to out-do any English duke. The 'disgraceful littleness' of the royal palaces in London had been a subject of critical comment by foreigners and Englishmen alike for over a century. When the allied sovereigns had visited England following the defeat of Napoleonic France, the absence of anywhere appropriate to house them had been the cause of national embarrassment. The position had been made even worse as a result of the destruction by a fire of a substantial proportion of St James's Palace in 1804, including the private apartments at the south-east corner.

Following Queen Charlotte's death in 1818, the Prince had cast covetous eyes on the Queen's House as the most suitable of the existing royal palaces in

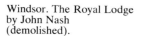

Windsor. The Royal Lodge by John Nash (demolished).

London for conversion into a modern palace, but the Prime Minister, Lord Liverpool, refused to make any money available for new state rooms. The sale of the site of St James's Palace to raise money was considered, but there was a change of mind, and as an interim measure in 1821 George IV embarked on a reconstruction of the St James's state rooms as the only place capable of housing the court on great occasions. As usual with George IV's building works, things rapidly got out of hand, and by 1822 £25,000 had been spent; by 1824 the cost had risen to £60,000.[18] The south front was extended in the old manner in dark brick with a crenellated parapet and a decent open courtyard, Friary Court, formed where the burnt-out buildings had been demolished. Inside the new range was a large new drawing room, called Queen Anne's Room, connected with the old state rooms, which were redecorated to match with gilded stucco ceilings and brought-in older fittings including chimneypieces by William Kent from Queen Caroline's Library (demolished 1825) and from Kensington Palace. Much of this work was done under the supervision of Sir Charles Long, and the decorative marbling on the walls of the remodelled main staircase was copied from his own house at Bromley Hill, Kent.[19]

Before the state rooms at St James's Palace had been completed, they were superseded by developments at Buckingham Palace. The King had first intended to modernize it as a private residence for use in conjunction with St James's, as in his father's day, but by 1826 he had decided to go the whole hog and convert it into a fully-fledged state palace where he could hold his courts and conduct the official business of the monarchy, though he never came entirely clean about his intentions when trying to get money out of his 'damned ministers'. He had, however, told Lord Liverpool that nothing short of £500,000 would do for the palace he had in mind, when offered £150,000 by the government.[20]

The work at Buckingham Palace should have been allotted to Sir John Soane as the Office of Works architect in charge of the Westminster palaces, not to mention the fact that he had been nursing ideas for the design of a neo-classical royal palace since his earliest youth, but at the King's instigation Soane was passed over and the commission was placed in Nash's hands. It was Nash who had the idea of providing the shortfall of money needed for a new palace by pulling down Carlton House and developing the site. Many of the fittings were salvaged for re-incorporation in the new rooms at Buckingham Palace and Windsor Castle. The ambivalence of intention over the enlargement of Buckingham Palace was largely responsible for its architectural defects. Instead of demolishing the old house and starting from scratch to a unified design, Nash and his successors were forced by financial straits to keep and remodel the existing building. This together with the faint aura of financial chicanery which hung around Nash's building transactions brought the palace into disrepute with contemporaries and affected later views of its merits. In fact Nash's plan was in many ways an ingenious solution to a difficult architectural problem. The old wings were demolished and replaced by new ones to form a solid U-shape enclosing an open courtyard, the fourth side of which was finished by iron railings and a central triumphal arch influenced by Percier et Fontaine's arrangement at the Tuileries in Paris for Napoleon.

The old main block itself was remodelled to permit both a circuit of the state rooms and an axial approach to the Throne Room, which made the new state suite equally suitable for formal audiences and for more social court events. The key to this arrangement was the staircase, with a single straight flight broken at a half landing where one flight continues straight ahead while two curved arms

St James's, Friary Court.

Opposite: St James's. The Grand Staircase which was remodelled under the direction of Sir Charles Long, later Lord Farnborough.

Right: St James's. Queen Anne's Room, a new state room added 1822–4.

St James's. Chimneypiece
in the Council Chamber.

return to a balcony over the foot and the entrance to the Guard Room, Green
Drawing Room and Throne Room. Along the centre of the main block was a
wide picture gallery with beyond it a new range of state rooms – the Blue
Drawing Room, Music Room and White Drawing Room – along the garden
front. The exterior of Nash's palace, faced in Bath stone, is exquisitely detailed
in a Frenchy neo-classical manner expressive of George IV's personal taste and
making much use of sculptured panels and trophies, *oeils-de-boeuf*, and carved
festoons, while the main feature of the garden front was a domed semi-circular
bow. As in Holland's Brighton Pavilion, Rousseau's *Hôtel de Salm* in Paris
provided a source of inspiration, as did Gondouin's *École de Chirugie*.[21]

The interiors of the palace were progressively enriched by George IV, with
the advice of Sir Charles Long, to meet an increasing desire for opulence and
grandeur. The decoration was notable for its large-scale use of brightly coloured
scagliola, lapis blue and raspberry pink, which Creevey thought made one feel
bilious just to look at; the use of sculptured panels in high places, which like the
marble chimneypieces were by leading sculptors including Westmacott, Rossi,
Carew, Sievier, Baily and M. C. Wyatt; and elaborately decorated ceilings
developed from those of Nash's Music Room and Dining Room at Brighton.
Much of the detailing was wildly eclectic and owed as much to the Italian
quattrocento, even to the Gothic, as to English or French neo-classical models.

Buckingham Palace. The entrance front as first built by Nash.

Buckingham Palace and the Marble Arch. This shows how Nash's design was altered and completed by Blore. Dr Waagen thought it looked 'as if some wicked magician had suddenly transformed some capricious stage machinery into solid reality'.

The Blue, White and Green Drawing Rooms, the Music Room and Throne Room are among the most original as well as the most opulent state rooms of their date. The Picture Gallery in the middle with its classical hammerbeam roof, influenced perhaps by Soane, was less successful, and despite its ingenuity failed to throw light on to the pictures, with the result that it has since been remodelled.

Nash wildly exceeded all the original estimates. By 1830 when George IV died it emerged that £501,530 had been spent. The Treasury initiated an investigation into the conduct of the building work and also into various structural and design defects. The result was that Nash was found guilty of 'inexcusable irregularity and great negligence' and disappeared from the scene. The completion of the palace was entrusted by William IV to Edward Blore, a more competent but far less inspired architect, and from 1832 he altered the roof, completed the forecourt and marble arch to a simpler design, and filled in the recessions on the garden front to create the State Dining Room and other additional apartments. In general he kept to the lines of Nash's design, but made it more solid and less Picturesque by ironing out the projections and recessions, and lopping the much criticized dome and 'turrets' from the roof line.[22]

George IV's palace-building in London therefore fizzled out somewhat

Buckingham Palace, Plan
of the Principal Floor in
1840

1 *Grand Staircase*
2 *Guard Chamber*
3 *Green Drawing Room*
4 *Throne Room*
5 *Picture Gallery*
6 *State Dining Room*
7 *Blue Drawing Room*
8 *Music Room*
9 *White Drawing Room*
10 *Private Apartments*

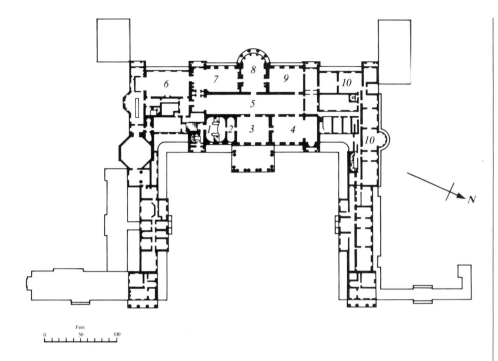

Buckingham Palace. The
Grand Staircase. The walls
were originally lined with
scagliola.

Right: Buckingham Palace. The Blue Drawing Room.

Below: Buckingham Palace. The Music Room. The columns are of lapis lazuli scagliola.

Bottom: Buckingham Palace. The White Drawing Room. The pilasters, originally of Sienna scagliola, were Frenchified by C. H. Bessant.

ignominiously with his architect Nash's censure and disgrace. The outcome at Windsor Castle was more successful, and George IV transformed it into the principal seat of the English monarchy at a cost of about a million pounds. Almost as soon as his father was dead, he started to plan moving from the Royal Lodge to the Castle and began preparations for continuing the Gothic restoration begun by James Wyatt nearly thirty years before. Sir Charles Long advised on the main lines of the proposed restoration. It was decided in 1823 to hold a competition for the work, and Long drew up an informal brief which determined the future character of the Castle, the heightening of the Round Tower, the enhancing of the silhouette, the addition of the Grand Corridor and creation of the Waterloo Chamber, the continuing of the Long Walk up to the Castle and the making of the George IV Gateway.[23] The three architects attached to the Office of Works, Soane, Smirke and Nash, together with James Wyatt's nephew and pupil, Jeffry, were asked to submit plans, and the job was awarded to the latter, who carried out Long's programme down to the last detail, earning a knighthood and the medievalizing of his surname to Wyatville.

The result is a masterpiece of Picturesque Gothic, with a splendid skyline which composes perfectly from every angle in all distant views. Unfortunately

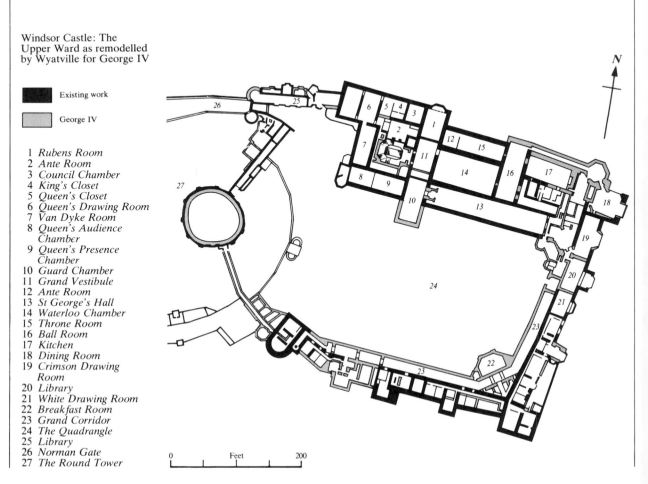

Windsor Castle: The Upper Ward as remodelled by Wyatville for George IV

N

Existing work

George IV

1 Rubens Room
2 Ante Room
3 Council Chamber
4 King's Closet
5 Queen's Closet
6 Queen's Drawing Room
7 Van Dyke Room
8 Queen's Audience Chamber
9 Queen's Presence Chamber
10 Guard Chamber
11 Grand Vestibule
12 Ante Room
13 St George's Hall
14 Waterloo Chamber
15 Throne Room
16 Ball Room
17 Kitchen
18 Dining Room
19 Crimson Drawing Room
20 Library
21 White Drawing Room
22 Breakfast Room
23 Grand Corridor
24 The Quadrangle
25 Library
26 Norman Gate
27 The Round Tower

0   Feet   200

Windsor Castle. The North side showing Wyatville's heightening of the sky line.

Sir Jeffry Wyatville was an architect of more competence than genius, and much of his close-up detail is frankly rebarbative, with ugly galletted pointing, clumsy machicolations, and harsh yellow masonry round the windows. The drastic alterations of Charles II's state rooms, which George III had carefully conserved, are also to be regretted, especially the destruction of St George's Hall and the Chapel, hitherto the finest baroque interiors in England. The new King's rooms on the east front, however, are magnificent, and the White, Crimson and Green Drawing Rooms, together with the Gothic Dining Room, are splendid palace rooms and fully compensate for the loss of those at Carlton House, many of the fittings from which they incorporate, including eleven pairs of Edward Wyatt's carved and gilt doors. The Grand Reception Room, too, with its white and gold plasterwork and Gobelin tapestries, is admirable, and the finest example of early nineteenth-century 'Louis Quatorze'. The Grand Corridor over 500 feet long with its seemingly endless vistas, its subdivision and exciting changes of direction, is the exact indoor equivalent of Nash's Picturesque street planning in Regent Street, as well as being an enormous asset to the comfort and convenience of the Castle.

George IV's work at Windsor was not restricted to the Castle itself but

Windsor Castle. The White
Drawing Room with doors
and chimneypiece from
Carlton House.

Opposite left: Windsor
Castle. Sir Jeffry
Wyatville's design for the
White Drawing Room.

Opposite right: Windsor
Castle. The Upper Ward
with the outside of the
Grand Corridor and the
private entrance.

Opposite below: Windsor
Castle. The Grand
Corridor.

involved considerable out-works in the Great Park and elsewhere, including
new lodges and lesser buildings. Three miles to the south at the end of the Long
Walk, and on axis with the new George IV gateway, he erected a large bronze
equestrian statue by Westmacott of George III on a high rocky plinth designed
by Wyatville. On the banks of the Long Water he arranged an artificial ruin
composed of genuine Roman columns from Leptis Magna in North Africa and
also built a Chinese Fishing Pavilion decorated by Crace with brightly coloured
trellis work and gilded dragons. It was in the park at Windsor, away from the
public gaze, that swollen with over-eating and dropsy he spent the last years of
his life, driving through the glades in a carriage or indolently fishing in the

Left: Windsor Castle. Sir Jeffry Wyatville's design for the entrance to the Coffee Room.

Right: Windsor Castle. St George's Hall. This enormously long room was formed by Wyatville out of the old hall and the chapel. The seemingly timber ceiling is of plaster.

afternoons from the verandah of the Chinese Pavilion. He died at Windsor in February 1830, leaving behind him an architectural achievement which filled the gap caused by eighteenth-century lethargy and lack of interest. His brother, who succeeded him as William IV, finished off the work at Windsor and Buckingham Palace as cheaply as possible, demolished the Royal Lodge, and at Brighton Pavilion removed the chandelier from the dining room for fear it might come loose from its moorings amidst the tobacco leaves and crash to the ground, annihilating the royal dining table and guests beneath.

X

VICTORIA AND ALBERT

Queen Victoria in the course of her long reign radically modified many of the traditions of her predecessors, and this affected the royal residences as much as any other aspect of the monarchy. In particular, she carried to its logical conclusion the division of the public and private sectors of the monarch's life begun under George III. She acquired two remote estates, one on the Isle of Wight and one in the Highlands of Scotland, and there built at her own expense two private houses distinct in ownership and architectural form from her official state palaces. In them she spent as much of her year immersed in private family life as she could force her reluctant ministers and public opinion to accept. For five hundred years the English monarchy had been based in south-east England, largely in the Thames valley, close to the seat of government at Westminster, but Queen Victoria broke away from this tradition and spent large portions of her life on an island off the coast of Hampshire and among the mountains and lochs of the Grampians, with just a minister in attendance to maintain the umbilical cord between the person of the monarch and the day-to-day machinery of her government in London. She was able to do this because of two dramatic changes which took place in her lifetime. One of these was the revolutionary improvement in transport in the early years of the reign, brought about by the development of the railways. Journeys which a few years earlier had taken a week to perform could now be accomplished in under a day by train and steam yacht. The other great change in Victoria's reign was a significant diminution of the real political power of the monarch. This made the court less important than hitherto in the day-to-day business of government. In the early nineteenth century it had still played a significant role in the distribution of political office. In the course of Victoria's reign, however, the royal 'drawing rooms' and levees ceased to have any political significance and became purely formal social events, while the monarch's role in the government was largely reduced to titular control only; fully-fledged constitutional monarchy had arrived.

On her accession to the throne in 1837 Victoria moved immediately into Buckingham Palace from Kensington, where she had been brought up by her German mother, the widowed Duchess of Kent, a Princess of Saxe-Coburg. George IV's new palace had only just been completed and William IV had never lived there, death having removed him before the final touches could be added. Though fresh from the hands of the builders, the new palace was far from perfect. Endless small improvements and alterations proved necessary to make it comfortably habitable: in particular, the enhancement of the privacy of her own rooms and the making good the omission of a private chapel. The inadequacies of the new palace became even more obvious following the Queen's marriage to her cousin, Prince Albert of Saxe-Coburg, in 1840. The root of the trouble was that the palace was too small, both for state functions and for family life. Splendid though George IV's state apartments were, none of them was big enough for a court ball. Equally serious for a newly married couple was the absence of any nurseries. Moreover, there were not enough bedrooms for visitors, and the kitchens were old-fashioned and badly planned. The obvious solution was to make the palace a complete quadrangle by closing the east side of the courtyard with a new wing. This scheme was adopted, and entailed the removal of the Marble Arch to the north-east corner of Hyde Park; it was in any case too narrow for the state coach to pass through, thanks to Nash's slapdash methods of designing. The new range, with the necessary apartments for distinguished visitors on the first floor and nurseries on top, was designed by Edward Blore, an architect chosen by the government because of his reputation for cheapness. It was built from 1847 to 1850 by Thomas Cubitt, the leading builder of the day, who had recently established his reputation by the development of the Grosvenor estate to the west of the palace into the handsome residential districts of Pimlico and Belgravia.[1] Rather sadly, Blore's new front made no effort to relate either stylistically or in its materials to Nash's original architecture and thus spoilt the unity of George IV's palace (a fault

Buckingham Palace. The new façade added by Edward Blore in 1847–50.

Buckingham Palace. The Grand Hall in 1889 showing the walls lined with scagliola and the ceiling as decorated by Professor Ludwig Grüner.

Left: Buckingham Palace. Queen Victoria's Sitting Room in 1889.

Right: Buckingham Palace. Prince Albert's Sitting Room in 1889.

perpetuated by Aston Webb's Edwardian remodelling of Blore's Façade, though in every other way that is infinitely superior to its predecessor). Blore's architecture was an uninspired Classical, reminiscent of an English railway hotel or a minor German princely palace, and was an altogether dowdy performance compared to George IV's stylish Francophile garden front. It was not greatly admired at the time of its completion. *The Builder*, for instance, in 1847 remarked that it 'does not pretend to grandeur and magnificence, scarcely to dignity'. It was a lost architectural opportunity, and its replacement is not to be regretted. Part of the trouble was a very tight budget, and the new wing had to be paid for partly by selling Brighton Pavilion. In fitting up the new rooms inside, Blore, against his wishes, was forced to draw heavily on the fittings and furnishings of the dismantled Pavilion, creating a series of unlikely Early Victorian Chinese rooms including the East Room and the Luncheon Room.

The extension of the suite of state apartments along the west front of the palace by the addition at the south end of new galleries, a State Supper Room and a huge Ballroom 123 feet long and 60 feet wide was entrusted to a different architect, Nash's pupil James Pennethorne. Blore had not been admired as an architect by Prince Albert, and his failure to please his royal clients upset him to the extent that he refused the Knighthood offered to him on the completion of the work. The new south-west block was built in 1852 to 1855 by Thomas

Cubitt. The exterior is an admirable paraphrase of Nash's style and harmonizes perfectly with George IV's garden front, though it upsets the original symmetry. The high quality of the interior was a direct result of the intervention of Prince Albert and was an expression of his cultivated international taste. The work was executed by artists of his own choice under his personal supervision, as was nearly every other royal architectural project of any consequence carried out during his lifetime. The Ballroom was given an elaborate polychrome scheme designed by Ludwig Grüner, a German Professor of Art from Dresden, who was appointed artistic designer to Prince Albert in 1845. The upper parts of the walls were covered with large paintings of the twelve hours by Niccola Consoni, a Roman artist whose best-known works are the murals in the basilica of St Paul's Outside the Walls. Over the doors were placed groups carved by William Theed, a sculptor admired by Prince Albert. Much of this decoration has now disappeared, but some of Grüner, Consoni and Theed's work survives in the adjoining galleries.[2]

Grüner was responsible for a whole series of rich polychrome Italianate decorative schemes in the different royal palaces, only parts of which now survive fortunately including some very handsome carpets in the private drawing rooms at Windsor. His most attractive ensemble fell victim to dry rot earlier this century. This was the Swiss Cottage or 'Mound Pavilion' built in the garden at Buckingham Palace by Prince Albert. The octagonal domed sitting room inside was embellished by eight Royal Academicians with paintings illustrating scenes from Milton's *Comus* in a setting of Raphaelesque grotteschi on an apple green ground painted by Grüner, the whole being done under his general supervision.[3]

As has been seen, the improvements to Buckingham Palace in the 1840s were partly financed by the sale of Brighton Pavilion. Queen Victoria on a visit to Brighton at the beginning of her reign had quickly come to the decision that she did not like the place. Its almost total lack of privacy was insupportable. It was not possible to walk about without being stared at. The Pavilion occupied a constricted site in the middle of what was rapidly expanding into a popular seaside town of a very different character from the select late-Georgian resort which George IV had known. The building itself was in every way unsuitable as a holiday home for a growing family. The Queen immediately decided to dispose of it and to buy an alternative, more secluded seaside house better adapted to quiet family life. Her thoughts turned to the Isle of Wight which she had first visited in 1831. On that occasion she had stayed at Norris Castle with her mother and two Würtemberg cousins, and they had been visited there by the Queen of Portugal (who politely accepted the somewhat rebarbative gift of an album of pressed seaweed). Victoria had revisited Norris Castle in 1833 and much enjoyed herself. So when she was looking for 'a place of one's own quiet and retired' to replace Brighton, it was to the Isle of Wight that her attention turned.

The Prime Minister, Sir Robert Peel, sympathetically promoted her inquiries and led her to Osborne on the north side of the island, overlooking the Solent. Its situation was not too inconvenient for London, and it had all the characteristics which the Queen required, seclusion, proximity to the sea, and a private beach for bathing and boating. Victoria and Albert paid a trial visit in 1843 and found it enchanting. The setting reminded Albert of Naples, and Victoria wrote: 'It is impossible to imagine a prettier spot – we have a charming beach quite to ourselves – we can walk anywhere without being followed or mobbed.' She was determined to purchase, and in 1845 she bought the Osborne estate from Lady

Osborne in the 1880s showing the Household Wing on the left.

Isabella Blachford. This initial thousand acres was subsequently enlarged by buying the Barton estate from Winchester College and other farms from neighbouring landowners. At first the Queen intended to keep the existing Osborne House, a comfortable plain Georgian affair, but on Cubitt's advice it was decided to demolish outright and to build a completely new house on the site. The Queen was delighted to have somewhere which was entirely her own property, and where she could please herself without having to struggle with various inefficient government departments. She wrote to Uncle Leopold on 20 March 1845, 'You will, I am sure be pleased to hear we have succeeded in purchasing Osborne . . . It sounds so snug and nice to have a place of *one's own*, quiet and retired, and free from all Woods and Forests and other charming Departments who are really the plague of one's life.'[4]

In the development of the estate and the design of the new house Queen Victoria was happy to give Prince Albert a free hand, as at Buckingham Palace. It is his taste and knowledge rather than hers which is reflected in all the architectural projects of the reign, for even after his death the Queen continued to be influenced by what she thought he would have chosen and continued to rely on the artists, architects and advisers whom her husband had admired. At Osborne the new house was built by Thomas Cubitt under Prince Albert's immediate supervision with no other architect involved, though Professor Grüner advised on all the interior decoration. The fruit of this Anglo-German collaboration is an Italianate villa with two belvedere towers, of the type invented by Sir Charles Barry at Mount Felix and Trentham. It is a light and cheerful building, brilliantly asymmetrical in layout, the detail an harmonious assemblage of Palladian, Florentine and Roman motifs. Osborne made an enormous impact on the architecture of the time and was widely copied both in England and abroad. It became a favourite model both for manufacturers' villas and princely summer palaces.

The most extraordinary aspect of Osborne is the plan, with a compact pavilion for the royal family's own occupation, and the large asymmetrical east wing, attached only by the corridor, for the accommodation of the royal household,

Osborne showing the Family Pavilion before the addition of the Durbar Room in 1890.

government ministers and other visitors. No other palace has such a plan, but the inspiration for the semi-detached arrangement of buildings for the household may have derived from the German practice of building a little *residenz-stadt* adjoining the royal palace to provide accommodation for courtiers, guests, soldiers and so forth. The brilliant innovation at Osborne was to link all the different building conveniently together under one roof while maintaining the cosy 'small private house' independence of the Family Pavilion for Queen Victoria's own occupation. The foundation stone of the Family Pavilion was laid on 23 June 1845 and the shell completed by the end of that year. The interior fitting up was done the following year and the house was ready for occupation by September 1846. The old house adjoining was then demolished to make way for the semi-detached Household Wing to the east, which was completed in 1851. The terrace gardens, as Italianate as the house, were designed by Prince Albert in 1847 and helped frame the splendid views down to the sea and over the Solent to Spithead, where the ships of the Royal Navy could frequently be seen riding at anchor.

The Family Pavilion was handsomely decorated under Grüner's direction. Perhaps the most impressive interior was the Marble Corridor, a spacious U-shaped gallery linking together the different parts of the house and no doubt inspired by Wyatville's Grand Corridor at Windsor. It was painted by Messrs Moxon and Muller with marbled pilasters and polychrome stencilling in strong Classical colours: black, red, umber and blue. The floor was paved with Minton encaustic tiles in equally strong colours designed by Prince Albert. Inset into the walls were casts of the Parthenon frieze, and spaced at intervals along the gallery's length were the Prince's discriminating purchases of contemporary sculpture, especially the work of artists living in Rome, Pietro Tenerani, John Gibson, and R. J. Wyatt, some of whose statues were also bought for Windsor and Buckingham Palace. In theory these were placed on revolving pedestals so that they could be turned to advantage in different light, but two bored young equerries on duty in the Corridor in the 1890s discovered to their horror that the pivots did not work, when they tried to revolve Psyche and she fell slowly into

Osborne House, Isle of
Wight, Ground Floor

1 *Drawing Room*
2 *Billiard Room*
3 *Dining Room*
4 *Principal Staircase*
5 *Corridor*
6 *Vestibule*
7 *Marble Corridor*
8 *Council Chamber*
9 *Duchess of Kent's Suite*
10 *Household and Main
Wing*

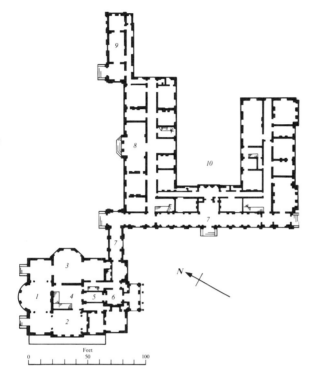

Osborne, the Marble
Corridor decorated by
Messrs Moxon & Muller
under Professor Grüner's
direction.

their arms; it needed all their strength to lower her without damaging the tiled floor. Footmen were summoned to no avail, and it required a crane to replace her on her pedestal. The following day the Queen sent a severe note to all members of the Household saying that they were not to play with the statues.

The ground floor of the Family Pavilion was occupied almost entirely by the three principal rooms, the Billiard Room, the Drawing Room, and the Dining Room. These large attractive rooms were filled with light from the tall plate glass windows, an effect keenly appreciated by Prince Albert. Queen Victoria later wrote to her eldest daughter, the Empress Frederick of Germany, 'dear Papa disliked all the English country seats [he] said they were all made so dark and with our vy dark & dull climate every thing shld be light and bright as here [Balmoral] and at Osborne.'⁵ The Billiard Room and the Drawing Room were separated only by a screen of yellow marble Corinthian columns, and formed in effect one large L-shaped room. But the problem of the men having to stand in the Queen's presence was solved by having the table round the corner, out of sight of the Queen and her ladies, so that the men could sit round it to watch the game. Prince Albert was very fond of billiards and he himself designed the table, which was made by Moxons and decorated by Thurston. Much of the other furniture in the house was provided by Hollands.

The Drawing Room had the central bow window with fine views over the terraces and park towards the Solent. It was decorated with enriched and gilded plasterwork and filled with rich furniture and objects, portraits by Winterhalter, and vases given by Tsar Nicolas I, Pope Pius IX, and other foreign heads of state. The main staircase in the middle of the Family Pavilion was frescoed by Dyce with Neptune entrusting the Command of the Sea to Britannia. It gave access to the private suite of the Queen and Prince Albert on the first floor comprising a sitting room, bedroom, two dressing rooms and two fitted bathrooms. The technology throughout the house was remarkably advanced; the construction was largely of cast-iron and fireproof, and the plumbing, central heating and other services were all of the most modern kind and did credit to Cubitt's practical sense. On the top floor above Queen Victoria and Prince Albert's apartments were the nurseries for the royal children. They also had a Swiss Cottage in the grounds, and their own little gardens where they could learn to grow flowers and vegetables as part of Prince Albert's rather Germanic programme for their education. Their spades and wheelbarrows are still preserved, each marked with its owner's initials.

The Queen spent as much time as she could with her family at Osborne, away from affairs of state. She stated her priorities in a letter of 1846: 'Really when one is so happy and blessed in one's home life, as I am, politics (providing my country is safe) must take second place.'⁶ She was determined to have a private life of her own away from the government, Windsor and Buckingham Palace. This desire for seclusion increased after Albert's death, and she spent longer portions of the year at Osborne in deepest mourning. The reaction of guests and courtiers varied. Greville, the rather supercilious clerk of the Privy Council, dismissed it as being 'like a small German Principality Palace'. Others dreaded the 'royal game of summer' at Osborne, Queen Victoria being more impervious to cold than most of those round her. She would sit in chilly weather with all the windows wide open and everybody blue with cold, and then express the doubt that perhaps it was too hot to go out. On the occasional day of real summer weather it could, however, be charming, with the sunlight sparkling on the sea and the smell of jasmine on the terraces. Disraeli with typical exaggeration

Osborne, the Billiard Room. The billiard table was designed by Prince Albert.

Osborne, the Council Chamber, a concession to the Queen's official public life.

Osborne, the Durbar
Room added in 1890. The
Indian decoration was
designed by Bhai Ram
Singh.

described it as 'a Sicilian Palazzo with garden terraces, statues and vases shining
in the sun, than which nothing can be conceived more captivating'. The
characteristic vignette of the Queen at Osborne in old age is at breakfast, sitting
in a green fringed tent in the park surrounded by Indian servants and highland
dogs, with everything on the table, except her cup and saucer but including her
egg cup, of solid gold.

As she grew older, and especially after becoming Empress of India in 1876,
the Queen developed a strong interest in Indian things, and surrounded herself
with Indian servants such as the slightly disreputable Munshi (with his good-
looking 'nephews') who succeeded John Brown as her favourite personal
servant. Thus when it came to adding a large new reception hall to replace the
inconvenient temporary marquee on the west side of the Family Pavilion at
Osborne, the Indian style was chosen and the room was called the Durbar Hall.
It was very different in feel from the Prince Regent's 'Indian' architecture at
Brighton. This was very serious and very solid. The building work was executed
by Cubitt's from sketches prepared by the Queen's estate surveyor, but the
interior decoration was done under the supervision of Bhai Ram Singh, an
expert on Indian architecture and decoration; and John Lockwood Kipling, the
director of the Lahore Central Museum and father of Rudyard Kipling, was
consulted about the initial design. The Durbar Hall with its teak dado and

fretted Moghul plasterwork proved the perfect setting for the various gifts from 'Eastern Potentates' received by the Queen on the occasion of her two Jubilees. The total effect is like a pavilion at one of the late nineteenth or early twentieth-century international trade exhibitions. At the same time as the addition of the Durbar Hall in 1890, electric light was installed throughout Osborne, supplied from accumulators in a battery-house erected near the Servants' Barracks. These were charged when necessary by a gas-driven generator. So Osborne continued to maintain its position in the forefront of domestic technology throughout Queen Victoria's reign.[7]

Although Queen Victoria and Prince Albert were so contented and busy at Osborne in the mid-1840s, they also developed in the same years a love-affair with Scotland, the scenery of which reminded the Prince of parts of Germany. Following the union of the English and Scottish Crowns, no monarch of the United Kingdom had resided regularly in Scotland, though Charles II had rebuilt Holyroodhouse in Edinburgh. George IV, however, had paid a state visit to Scotland in 1822 which was stage-managed by Sir Walter Scott, and the King had had his portrait painted wearing the kilt (and flesh-coloured tights) by Sir David Wilkie. This revival of royal interest in Scotland, stimulated by the writings of Sir Walter Scott and the Romantic interest in Picturesque landscape, was the background to Queen Victoria's own life-long infatuation with the Highlands. She first saw them in 1842 on a visit to the Marquis of Breadalbane at Taymouth Castle. Two years later she stayed at Blair Atholl and wrote, 'I can only say that the scenery is lovely, grand romantic, etc. a great peace and wildness pervades all which is sublime.'[8] In August 1847, the royal couple went on a holiday in the royal yacht up the west coast of Scotland and stayed at Ardverikie Lodge, a house decorated with frescoes by Landseer and with antlers everywhere. It rained and rained all the time, but while there, they heard of Balmoral, a property of the Earl of Fife on upper Deeside, which was reputed to be one of the driest parts of Scotland. The upshot of this was that the Queen took a thirteen-year lease of the property unseen, visiting it for the first time in September 1848.

The existing house at Balmoral had been built nine years before to the design of John Smith, an architect of Aberdeen nicknamed 'Tudor Johnnie'. The Queen was charmed by it: 'a pretty little Castle in the old Scotch style . . . one enters a nice little hall, & a billiard-room & Dining-room. A good broad staircase takes one upstairs & above the Dining-room is our sitting room . . . a fine large room opening into our bedroom etc.'

This first holiday at Balmoral was a roaring success, and the Queen and the Prince enjoyed themselves thoroughly, even if dinner was made late one evening 'owing to Albert's struggle to dress in his kilt'. He stalked. She sketched. 'Oh! What can equal the beauties of nature! What enjoyment there is in them! Albert enjoys it so much! he is in ecstasies here.' The royal household, however, saw it all through slightly less rose-tinted spectacles. The midges were insupportable. The Highlanders were nearly always drunk on whisky. Everybody except the royal family had to camp out in nearby cottages, and their breakfast was sent over to them from the big house in wheelbarrows. The grumbles of courtiers and ministers at the discomfort and inconvenience of it all runs like a refrain through Queen Victoria's life at Balmoral, the counterpoint to her own ecstasies. Balmoral, however, received the approbation of one unlikely critic. Charles Greville, who visited it during that first autumn, confided to his journal: 'Much as I dislike Courts and all that appertains to them, I am glad to have made this expedition, and to have seen the Queen and Prince in their Highland retreat, where they certainly appear to great advantage. The place is very pretty, the house very small. They live there without any state whatever; they live not merely like private gentlefolks, but like very small gentlefolks . . .'⁹ By royal standards Balmoral was agreeably informal, and Victoria and Albert were thrilled with it and determined to make it a permanent holiday home, even more private and secluded than Osborne.

The Balmoral estate was bought outright in 1852, and the roughly concurrent purchases of Birkhall and Abergeldie made up a total holding of 30,000 acres, a respectable estate even by Scottish standards. In the same year the Queen was left a fortune by an eccentric miser, John Camden Nield, because he knew she 'would not waste it', and it was decided to use part of this money to rebuild Balmoral Castle. 'Tudor Johnnie' was now dead, but his son William Smith was an architect and so he was appointed for the job though, as at Osborne, the Prince's ideas were the dominant force. Smith was merely the executant, rather as A. J. Humbert was for Whippingham Church, which the Prince designed for the Osborne estate. Even when he employed an architect, the Prince liked to express his own ideas. A new site was chosen 100 yards from the old one in order to take better advantage of the views. The Prince made rough sketches of the prepared layout which he handed to Smith to make into finished designs. The overall plan was carefully thought out, with the main block, servants' block, stables and offices, including capacious game and venison larders, all in carefully marshalled formations. Because of the slope in the ground it was possible to place the subsidiary domestic parts at a lower level than the main block and to screen them from the dining room windows by the single-storeyed ballroom, 68 feet long and 25 feet wide. It was intended for the 'ghillies dances', which are still a feature of the Balmoral scene.¹⁰

The Prince told his architect that the building should be 'not like a palace, but like a country gentleman's house'. Despite this intended informality, it was still necessary to design accommodation for a hundred people – the domestic household staff and the Queen's Household-in-Waiting, comprising two Ladies-in-Waiting and two Maids of Honour (each with a ladies' maid), a Minister in Attendance, the Keeper of the Privy Purse, the Master of the Household, a Lord-in-Waiting and a Groom-in-Waiting, two Equerries and a Gentleman Usher (each with a man servant), plus the royal family and friends. Queen Victoria laid the foundation stone in 1853 and, as at Osborne, work proceeded rapidly. Local granite and local labour were used, though the carved work on the outside – heraldry and bas relief of subjects chosen by the Prince Consort – was done by John Thomas of London; the furniture was provided by Hollands, and hot and cold baths by Cubitt. The main block was ready for habitation in September 1855, and work then started on the subsidiary wings. As at Osborne, all the domestic technology was the last word in modernity: the construction was fireproof; there was hot air heating, four fitted bathrooms for the use of the royal family, and no fewer than fourteen W.C.'s elsewhere in the house, then the British record for a country house. The principal rooms, all 15 feet high, consisted of a library, drawing room and dining room, with the billiard room beyond, the Queen and the Prince's rooms above (as in the old house), while rooms for distinguished visitors and the Minister in Attendance were provided on the south side of the ground floor. The latter was the only concession at Balmoral to the Queen's public life. Although at Osborne there was an Audience Chamber in the corner of the Family Pavilion, as well as a splendid

Balmoral Castle, designed by Prince Albert and William Smith in 1853.

Council Room in the Household Wing, there was nothing of the kind at Balmoral. The castle was emphatically a private holiday home of the royal family. The interior was light and bright, with cheerful colours and much decorative use of tartan for wallpapers, chintzes and even for carpets. This was supplemented by a plentiful array of Scotch thistles ('They would rejoice the heart of a donkey' thought Lord Clarendon) and sporting trophies described by one of Queen Victoria's grandchildren as 'more patriotic than artistic'. The dining room, for instance, had green walls and red curtains. And in addition to the Royal Stuart and Hunting Stuart tartans, Prince Albert designed a Balmoral tartan prettily composed of shades of lilac, red and black. Rather oddly, the library seems to have been used as a family dining room on many occasions rather than the real dining room.

From the mid-1850s there began the regular routine of autumn migrations of the royal family to Balmoral. After Albert died the Queen's visits became longer, and she stayed from August to November in 'dear Albert's own creation' as well as two weeks in June. She spent the early summer at Osborne and otherwise was at Windsor, hardly ever going to London in the later part of the reign. Buckingham Palace was kept shut up and under dust covers. Balmoral was monstrously inconvenient for her Ministers, even with trains, but the Queen was determined to keep her privacy, her own houses, and the right to move around when and how she wished. Much of her time was spent in defending these rights against her Ministers, Lord John Russell, Palmerston, and Gladstone, not to mention the Press and the public, but she won and kept her own life. Ironically, perhaps, the fiercely private family life of the Queen at Balmoral is almost more famous and more written about than any other aspect of any monarch's life. The Queen's own *Journal of Our Life in the Highlands* describes it all, and hardly a year goes by without another book appearing on the subject. Every detail is well-known – the fishing, the stalking, the heather, the 'whist, whisky and midges', the picnics of cold meat and boiled potatoes, the energetic fifteen-mile walks, the memorial cairns, the ghillies' dances, John Brown's chapped legs and barked shins, and the tearful departures for the south. 'The Queen has returned to her usual devoted, passionate admiration for the Highlands. Leaving them is always a case of actual *red eyes*.'[11]

When at Windsor 'fine as it is', the Queen wrote, 'I long for our cheerful and unpalace-like rooms at Osborne and Balmoral', and she tends to be associated in retrospect exclusively with those two private houses; but the greatest portion of each year was spent at Windsor, which for the whole of her reign enjoyed the position of principal palace of the British monarchy and was therefore the focus of the British Empire as well as of nearly the whole of royal Europe. It was visited by heads of state from all over the world and was the scene of a series of

Windsor Castle.
The George IV Gateway
c. 1890; the windows of
Queen Victoria's private
apartments are protected
by blinds.

magnificent state visits. On these occasions the state apartments were brought back into use for the purpose for which they were designed and had so rarely been occupied in the past. The visit of Napoleon III and the Empress Eugenie in 1855 was especially successful, and on that occasion the late eighteenth-century state bed made by Georges Jacob was refurbished and given new purple and green hangings worked with the French Eagle and initials of the Emperor and Empress and trimmed with some of Queen Charlotte's floral needlework. Both the Emperor and the King of Italy were invested with the Order of the Garter by Queen Victoria in a splendid ceremony at Windsor that summer. It was in the reign of Queen Victoria that the Grand Corridor became notorious because of the time that Ministers and other officials had to spend in its under-heated length waiting to be summoned to audience, or after dinner on less formal occasions when the Queen would sit there talking to each guest in turn while the remainder of the company stood around trying to avoid the worst draughts or leant surreptitiously against the wall to rest their feet. And even today it is the shade of great Victorian statesmen, Gladstone or Disraeli, which lingers in the Prime Minister's Rooms rather than some more modern politician.

At the time that the Queen succeeded to the throne the restoration of Windsor was only just being completed, and when Wyatville died in 1840 he left the Upper Ward transformed into a palace worthy of the British monarchy,

Windsor Castle from the North *c.* 1890 with the Curfew Tower as reconstructed by Salvin in the 1860s.

Windsor Castle. The
Horseshoe Cloister and
Curfew Tower in 1870
before 'restoration'.

Windsor Castle. The
Horseshoe Cloister after
'restoration' by Sir Gilbert
Scott in 1871.

comfortable and convenient as well as magnificent, so few major alterations
were necessary in the course of the reign. The Queen did, however, carry out
further minor improvements. Blore contrived a little private chapel in the
polygonal space above the Visitors' Entrance and made an underground passage
between the Queen's apartments and the orangery overlooking the east garden.
Restoration work was also continued in the Lower Ward, and this included the
repair of the Chapel over the Tomb House behind St George's Chapel. This was
completed in the 1860s by Salvin, who also gave the Curfew Tower its
Carcassone-like profile and reconstructed Wyatville's staircase to the state
apartments (which in turn had superseded James Wyatt's for George III).
Lastly, Sir Gilbert Scott supervised the sweeping restoration of the
Horseshoe Cloisters at the west end of St George's Chapel in 1871. The major
Victorian alterations and improvements, however, took place in the grounds
and parks. It was there that Prince Albert expressed himself. His interests in

improving art, industry and the condition of the labouring classes all found the perfect outlet in agriculture at Windsor when he was appointed Ranger of the Great Park. He had been responsible for great improvements at Osborne and Balmoral, draining and making new roads, planting, fencing, erecting model farm buildings and new cottages. It was at Windsor, however, that he was able to improve on the largest scale. He moulded the Home Park into one continuous estate by combining the grounds of Frogmore and Shaw Farm, and by diverting the public road to Datchet round the northern perimeter when the railway was built. Magnificent new farm buildings were put up at Shaw Farm in 1853 in a grand Italianate style to the design of G. A. Dean, the leading farm architect of the day responsible for, among other things, the buildings at Longlands and the Model Farm at Holkham in Norfolk. The Home or Dairy Farm at Frogmore was also rebuilt in 1852 in a vague Tudorbethan style to the design of J. R. Turnbull, and six years later Prince Albert rebuilt George III's dairy, which had various practical defects, to Turnbull's design in what was called the 'Renaissance style'. The chief interest of the dairy is its interior, which is a perfect demonstration of the 'art-manufacture' which Prince Albert was so keen on promoting. All the interior decoration was designed by John Thomas, Prince Albert's favourite sculptor. The walls are completely covered with green and white Minton tiles and embellished with Minton's 'majolica' bas reliefs, while at either end are 'majolica' fountains designed by Thomas. The brightly painted roof is supported on six ornamental columns. The whole ensemble is the finest Victorian dairy interior in England and far outshines, as it was intended to, any of the country-house dairies which Queen Victoria and the Prince had visited on their tours of England and Scotland in the 1840s, such as those at Arundel and Taymouth Castles. New walled kitchen gardens extending to sixty acres, with enormous iron-framed greenhouses, were also built at Frogmore at the same time.[12]

In the Great Park, the Prince initiated a programme of rejuvenation of the Long Walk, replacing decayed or stunted elms with new trees, and also provided large numbers of new estate cottages, mainly designed by S. S. Teulon. The Prince was a keen promoter of good housing and embarked on a scheme at Windsor intended to ensure that every labourer on the royal estate was comfortably housed within one mile of his work. He also replaced George III's farm buildings at the Flemish Farm with a large new steading designed by J. R. Turnbull, though the Georgian timber buildings at the Norfolk Farm were retained and repaired. On the strength of his work at Windsor, the Prince was elected President of the Royal Agricultural Society but did not live long enough to take up the post. He died of typhoid fever at Windsor Castle on 14 December 1861, plunging Queen Victoria into lifelong grief.[13] After his death a sombre atmosphere permeated the castle and there was constantly the feeling that somebody was missing. In the manner of German mourning his rooms were left exactly as they were on the day of his death, with fresh water placed on the washstand daily.

The late-Victorian history of Windsor is largely that of erecting suitable memorials to Prince Albert. The chapel over the Tomb House was converted by the Queen into a glowing shrine to his memory, the Albert Memorial Chapel. The interior was stunningly remodelled from 1863 to 1873 by Sir Gilbert Scott and Baron H. de Trinqueti; the walls were lined with etched marble reliefs of biblical subjects by Jules Destréez, the vaults encrusted with golden mosaic by Salviati, and the windows filled with stained glass by Clayton & Bell. There is

Windsor Castle. The Albert Memorial Chapel before Gilbert's screen was added to the Duke of Clarence's Tomb.

nothing else like this in England, though there are parallels in France and Germany. It is rich, restrained, and deeply moving. As well as this cenotaph chapel, Queen Victoria also erected a mausoleum for her husband and herself at Frogmore. This was perhaps the most novel of the architectural changes initiated in her reign by the Queen. Hitherto the sovereigns of this country had been buried in ancient churches with royal associations. The Queen's immediate forerunners had been buried at St George's Chapel, Windsor. For herself and her husband, however, the Queen preferred to build a special tomb house in a private garden. Her decision was not the direct consequence of her husband's premature death, but the realization of a long-meditated plan which owed its origins to the Saxe-Coburg family in Germany from which both her mother and her husband came. Her uncle Leopold of Saxe-Coburg (later King of the Belgians) had, following the death of his wife Princess Charlotte, the only daughter of George IV, built a small Gothic mausoleum in the grounds of

Above right: Windsor Castle. Statue of Penelope commissioned by Prince Albert from R. J. Wyatt for the entrance to the Queen's apartments.

Above left: Frogmore. Design for the Royal Mausoleum by A. J. Humbert.

Claremont, and this gave Queen Victoria and Prince Albert the idea of building a mausoleum for themselves. In 1844 the Prince and his brothers erected such a mausoleum at Coburg for their father and his family. Queen Victoria's mother asked if she could be buried in a mausoleum at Coburg too. This was impractical, and so instead a mausoleum was built for her in the grounds of Frogmore. It was a rotunda of Penrhyn granite, designed by Ludwig Grüner and executed by A. J. Humbert in 1861, and it formed a trial run for the main royal mausoleum.

Following the death of the Prince Consort, Queen Victoria lost no time in carrying into effect her ideas for the royal mausoleum and chose a site for it close to her mother's at Frogmore. She employed the Prince's architects:

Grüner to make the designs and Humbert to carry them out in the years 1862–71. The exterior is Lombardic, the walls of granite and Portland stone. The roof is sheathed in Australian copper. Richly cast gunmetal doors give access to the splendid spectacle of the interior, which is in the richest Italian High Renaissance style embellished with marble and stencilled paintwork of red, dark blue and yellow. Round the walls are frescoes by German and Italian artists in the manner of Raphael, whom the Prince Consort had thought the greatest of all artists. Under the central dome is the sarcophagus of marble, bronze and flawless Aberdeen granite, with glistening white effigies of Prince Albert and Queen Victoria by Marochetti. The Queen's was executed at the same time as the Prince's and kept in store till her death in 1901, by which time it was so long since it had been made that there was some difficulty remembering where it was. Though executed after his death, the Royal Mausoleum at Frogmore is the finest expression of Prince Albert's personal taste, just as the Queen intended it to be. Though comparatively small in scale, it is among the two or three finest examples in Europe of mid-nineteenth-century Classical taste, comparable with Von Klenze's Hermitage extension in St Petersburg or St Paul's Outside the Walls in Rome. 'The Queen's grief still sobs through its interior as though she had left her sorrow on earth to haunt this rich, forbidding temple to her loneliness.'[14]

POSTSCRIPT

Sandringham, the latest in date of the houses of the British monarchy, is the least distinguished architecturally. The Norfolk estate, with its excellent partridge and pheasant shoot, was bought for the Prince of Wales, the future King Edward VII, in 1861. At first he retained the existing house, to which he made various alterations and additions in 1861–3. But in 1870 he decided to make a clean sweep. The old house was demolished and a new one begun to the design of the Prince Consort's tame architect, A. J. Humbert. Without the Prince's guidance, however, and without the help of Professor Grüner, Humbert made a pretty poor showing. The style of Sandringham is Jacobean, with gables, turrets, and mullion windows, executed in red brick with stone dressings, on the model of such old Norfolk houses as Blickling. The result is big and bleak. Additions were made in 1883 to the design of R. W. Edis, a better architect than Humbert, and his work has a good deal more vitality. These additions included the Ball Room, with flamboyant Jacobean-style plasterwork, and the Bowling Alley, modelled on one at Rumpelheim near Frankfurt, the seat of the Hesse-Cassel family. In 1891 a fire damaged the upper part of the house and a second storey was subsequently added by Edis, who also built a small house in the grounds, York Cottage, for the Duke of York, later George V, at the time of his marriage. Described by Harold Nicolson as 'this most nondescript villa', York Cottage was George V's favourite residence because its small cosy rooms reminded him of ships' cabins and his happy years as a midshipman in the Royal Navy. Following the death of Queen Victoria and the conversion of Osborne into a nursing home for naval officers, Sandringham became the chief private house of the English royal family.

In London Edward VII, as Prince of Wales, was given Marlborough House which had been built originally by Wren in 1709–11. It was successfully altered by Pennethorne, who added a top storey in the same style in 1861–3. On his accession to the throne in 1901, Edward VII moved to Buckingham Palace and made it, for perhaps the only time in its history, the centre of a socially glittering court. He immediately initiated a sweeping refurbishment of the interior under the direction of an obscure decorator called C. H. Bessant. This unfortunately involved the destruction of much of the Regency and early-Victorian poly-chrome decoration, the rich scagliola, and Grüner's decorative painting, and the substitution everywhere of commonplace white and gold, reminiscent of a smart hotel of the period. In the Grand Hall, for instance, the dark marbled

Sandringham. Design for the entrance front by A. J. Humbert.

Sandringham. The garden front.

walls and the coloured stencilling of the ceiling were whitened over. The same treatment was extended to the Marble Hall, Grand Staircase, vestibules, galleries, and the White Drawing Room, which were all painted white, heavily gilded, and embellished with finicky festoons, swags and other decorative motifs at odds with Nash's original detailing. The most unfortunate alteration was the destruction of Grüner's and Consoni's magnificent interior of the Ball Room. It was replaced by a weak white and gold Louis XVI scheme, with fluted Ionic pilasters and *oeils-de-boeuf* windows, which obliterated the original architectural quality of the room.

Some atonement for these destructive alterations was made by the work

Buckingham Palace in 1913 showing the refacing of the East range to the design of Aston Webb and his rearrangement of the forecourt railings.

Buckingham Palace. Aston Webb's East front.

carried out at Buckingham Palace under George V and Queen Mary, though the King himself had no more aesthetic sensibility than his father and at times expressed impatience with his wife's keen interest in furniture and decoration. George V's chief personal contribution to the works executed in his reign was the elimination of the proposed sculpture and urns on the parapet of Aston Webb's new east front of the palace. Blore had used soft Caen stone for the east range which turned out to be perishable in the London climate. It was therefore decided in 1913 to re-face the Blore front in Portland stone to a new design as a backdrop to the Queen Victoria Memorial and the culmination of the remodelled approach along the Mall planned in 1901. The work was done in three months without disturbing the existing glazing of the windows. Webb's design is a dignified and self-assured *Beaux Arts* classical, perfectly adapted to its purpose and drawing inspiration from Gabriel's elegant façades in the Place de la Concorde in Paris. It is due to Aston Webb that Buckingham Palace looks like a palace. Much of the architectural effect comes from the forecourt and new *rond point* in front, with magnificent gateways and railings, the gilded ironwork of which was made by the Bromsgrove Guild. Webb designed new gateposts in the forecourt, but the other carved stone piers which punctuate the railings are old ones re-used, including a group by Blore and four smaller ones with lion's heads and floral swags carved by Edward Wyatt for George III in 1800. The whole of the new façade, forecourt and approaches was completed by the outbreak of the First World War.

Queen Mary took a keen personal interest in the interiors of all the royal palaces and initiated many improvements and schemes of restoration. At Buckingham Palace she carried out a great deal of redecoration in what were then thought to be 'Georgian' colours, buff, celadon green and Chinese yellow. The only major internal structural alteration was the remodelling of the Picture Gallery in 1914 and the substitution of a simple segmental glazed ceiling for Nash's complicated and impractical arrangement. The Chinese decoration of some of Blore's rooms was also enhanced under the direction of Charles Allom, especially the Centre Room and Yellow Drawing Room, where old Chinese wallpapers and silk hangings found in store were installed. They had probably been bought originally by George IV for the Brighton Pavilion. Both at Buckingham Palace and Windsor Castle Queen Mary contrived new guest suites for important visitors and furnished them partly with new acquisitions of English Georgian and Regency furniture carefully chosen to complement the existing royal collections. At Holyroodhouse and Hampton Court too, much work was carried out aimed at restoring the original character of the rooms, some of which were hung with coloured brocades and embellished with silver sconces (copied from originals at Windsor) and their contents re-arranged. Perhaps Queen Mary's greatest contribution to the royal palaces, especially Windsor and Buckingham Palace, was the re-arrangement and restoration of their historic contents, re-assembling sets of chairs, for instance, which had been split up. The informed and historically accurate approach, initiated by Queen Mary, has conditioned the upkeep and presentation of the royal residences and their contents down to the present.

NOTES

I. THE EARLY MIDDLE AGES

1 H. M. Colvin, *History of the King's Works*, I (1963), pp. 1–5.
2 *Two Saxon Chronicles*, I, ed. Charles Plummer (1889), pp. 219–22.
3 W. R. Lethaby, 'The Palace of Westminster in the Eleventh and Twelfth Centuries', *Archaeologia*, LX (1906).
4 T. F. Tout, 'The Beginnings of a Modern Capital . . .' *Collected Papers*, III (Manchester, 1934).
5 *King's Works*, I, pp. 492–3.
6 *Ibid*, pp. 51–6, 81.
7 *Ibid*, II, pp. 1009–16.
8 *Ibid*, I, pp. 93–9, 121–5; Philip Howard, *Royal Residences* (1970), p. 84.
9 *King's Works*, I, pp. 497–500; *Vetusta Monumenta*, VI (1842).
10 *King's Works*, I, p. 127.
11 *King's Works*, I, pp. 950–3, 1012–14.
12 P.R.O., Close Rolls 1242–7, pp. 293.

II. THE LATER MIDDLE AGES

1 *King's Works*, I, pp. 241–3.
2 *Ibid*, 161, pp. 510–19, 549–50; *Vetusta Monumenta*, VI (1842).
3 Philip Howard, *Royal Residences* (1970), pp. 44–8.
4 *King's Works*, I, pp. 995–7, 515–9; Howard, *op. cit.*, p. 48.
5 W. H. St John Hope, *Windsor Castle*, I (1913), pp. 178–97; *King's Works*, II, pp 872–6; Elias Ashmole, *History of the Most Noble Order of the Garter* (1715).
6 *King's Works*, I, pp. 527–9; Howard, pp. 50–1.
7 St John Hope, I, pp. 506–20.
8 A. R. Myers, *The Household of Edward IV* (Manchester, 1959), pp. 4–5, 47.

III. THE TUDORS

1 B. M. Cotton MS, Titus B.1, f 455.
2 Ian Dunlop, *Palaces and Progresses of Elizabeth I* (1962), pp. 75–6.
3 *Ibid*, pp. 79–82.
4 J. W. Kirby, 'Building Work at Placentia, 1532–3 and 1543–4', *Transactions of the Greenwich and Lewisham Antiquarian Society*, V, VI (1954).
5 Dunlop, pp. 45–9.
6 *King's Works*, III, p. 43.
7 *Survey of London*, XIII, p. 10.
8 *Ibid*, p. 17.
9 Evelyn, 28 August 1688: 'So parted, and with much difficulty, by candle-light, walked over the Matted Gallery, as it is now with the mats and boards all taken up, so that we walked over the rafters. But strange to see what hard matter the plaister of Paris is, that is there taken up, as hard as stone! And pity to see Holbein's work in the ceiling blotted on, and whited over.'
10 *Royal Historical Society Transactions*, 2nd series IX, p. 236.
11 *Survey of London*, XIII, p. 61.
12 *Royal Historical Society Transactions*, 2nd series IX, p. 255.
13 *R.C.H.M. West London* (1925), pp. 128–32.
14 Count Lorenzo Magalotti, *Travels of Cosmo the Third Grand Duke of Tuscany, through England* (1821).
15 E. W. Brayley, *Topographical History of Surrey*, II (1850).

16 Following the death of Arundel's son-in-law, Lord Lumley, Nonsuch reverted to the Crown in 1592 and at the end of her life became one of Elizabeth I's favourite residences.
17 Philip Howard, *Royal Palaces* (1970), p. 101.
18 Dunlop, p. 115.
19 *Royal Historical Transactions, op. cit.*

IV. THE ROYAL HOUSEHOLD

1 G. R. Elton, 'The Tudor Revolution; A Reply', *Past and Present*, No. 29, Dec. 1964, p. 43.
2 G. R. Elton, *The Tudor Revolution in Government* (1959), Chapter 6.
3 J. M. Beattie, *The English Court in the Reign of George I* (Cambridge, 1967).
4 Society of Antiquaries, *A Collection of Ordinances . . . from King Edward III to King William and Queen Mary* (1790), p. 158.
5 *Household Ordinances*, p. 154.
6. Hugh Murray-Baillie, 'Etiquette and Planning of the State Apartments in Baroque Palaces', *Archaeologia* (1967), CI, pp. 172–9.
7 *Household Ordinances*, p. 361.
8 *Ibid*, p. 342.
9 Murray-Baillie, *op. cit.*
10 *Correspondence of the Family of Hatton . . . 1601–1704*, II, ed. E. M. Thompson, (Camden Society, 1878), p. 21.
11 Beattie, pp. 13–14.
12 Beattie, pp. 17–18.

V. THE STUART COURT

1 H. M. Colvin, *A Biographical Dictionary of British Architects* (1978), p. 468.
2 Stephen Orgel & Roy Strong, *Inigo Jones, The Theatre of The Stuart Court*, 2 vols. (1972).
3 Stephen Harrison, *Arches of Triumph* (1604).
4 John Harris, Stephen Orgel & Roy Strong, *The King's Arcadia: Inigo Jones and the Stuart Court* (Arts Council Exhibition Catalogue, 1973), p. 43.
5 Anthony van Wyngaerde drawings, Ashmolean Museum, Oxford.
6 H. Chettle, *The Queen's House Greenwich* (Survey of London, 1937).
7 *The King's Arcadia*, p. 99.
8 N. Pevsner, *London I* (1973), p. 534.
9 *Survey of London*, XIII, pp. 27, 120.
10 *Ibid*, p. 28.
11 *The King's Arcadia*, p. 118.
12 P.R.O., E 351/3268.
13 R.I.B.A.D.
14 *Ibid.*
15 *King's Arcadia*, p. 148.
16 P.R.O., E 351/3269.
17 *King's Arcadia*, p. 165.
18 *Survey of London*, XIII, p. 28.
19 Partly at Chatsworth and partly at Worcester College, Oxford.
20 Colvin, p. 469; Margaret Whinney, 'John Webb's Drawings for Whitehall Palace', *Walpole Soc.*, XXXI (1942–3).
21 Anon. *A deep sigh breath'd through the lodgings at White-Hall* (1642).
22 *Survey of London* XIII, pp. 31–3.

VI. THE RESTORATION

1 J. M. Beattie, *The English Court in the Reign of George I* (Cambridge, 1967), p. 106.
2 *Survey of London*, XIII, p. 99.
3 Count Lorenzo Magalotti, *Travels of Cosmo the Third Grand Duke of Tuscany, through England* . . . (1821), p. 171.
4 Devonshire Collection, Chatsworth, John Webb's designs for Whitehall; *Architectural Review*, June 1912, p. 347.
5 *Survey of London*, XIII, p. 75.
6 *Ibid*, p. 35.
7 *King's Works*, V, pp. 140–4.
8 Kerry Downes, *English Baroque Architecture* (1966), pp. 16–21.
9 R. S. Mylne, *The Master Masons to the Crown of Scotland* (1893), Chapters 9 & 10.
10 *King's Works*, V, pp. 304–12.
11 *Survey of London*, XIII, pp. 105–7; *King's Works*, V, p. 290.
12 *Survey of London*, XIII, p. 40.
13 *Ibid*, pp. 36–37.
14 R.C.H.M., *The Monuments of West London* (1925), pp. 68–71.
15 P.R.O., Works 6/14.
16 R.I.B.A.D., B4/1; *King's Works*, V, pp. 155–69.
17 P.R.O., Works 5/50–2.
18 *King's Works*, V, pp. 170–1.

VII. THE HANOVERIANS

1 Daniel Defoe, *A Tour thro' the Whole Island of Great Britain* . . . (1724–7) I, p. 357; John Gwynn, *London and Westminster Improved* (1766), pp. 10–11.
2 Philip Howard, *Royal Residences* (1970), p. 155.
3 *King's Works*, V, p. 178.
4 *Ibid*, p. 195; Royal Archives, Windsor Castle, Vanbrugh's design for Kensington Palace.
5 W. H. Pyne, *Royal Residences* (1819), II, p. 72.
6 Margaret Jourdain, *The Work of William Kent* (1948), pp. 38–62; *King's Works*, V, pp. 199–201.
7 Royal Archives, Windsor Castle, Portfolio 58, Vanbrugh's design for St James's Palace.
8 *King's Works*, V, pp. 230–3; *Vitruvius Britannicus*, (1767) IV, pls. 1–4. The quadrant wings were added by Princess Amelia to the design of Thomas Wright in the reign of George III. Subsequent royal occupants of White Lodge included Mary, Duchess of Gloucester, and the Duke and Duchess of Teck. In 1955 White Lodge became the Junior School of the Royal Ballet.
9 Horace Walpole, *Anecdotes of Painting*, ed. Dallaway, (1862), II, p. 564.
10 *Letters and Journals of Lady Mary Coke*, ed. J. A. Home (1892), p. 242.
11 Peter Willis, *Charles Bridgeman* (1977), pp. 97–8.
12 Walpole, *op. cit.*, III, p. 778.
13 Sir Edward Lovett Pearce's designs are in the Proby Collection at Elton Hall, Northamptonshire; William Kent's model is exhibited at the Dutch House at Kew.
14 Willis, *op. cit.*, p. 90, pp. 101–3.
15 John Harris, *Sir William Chambers* (1970), p. 33.
16 *Ibid*, pp. 32–8.

VIII. GEORGE III

1 John Brooke, *King George III* (1972).
2 John Harris, *Sir William Chambers* (1970), pp. 81–2.
3 Dorothy Stroud, *Capability Brown* (1950), p. 99. The royal gardens at Richmond form part of the Royal Botanical Garden at Kew.
4 Harris, p. 79; BM Add. MS 41134, p. 30.
5 Martin Miller, 'The Kew Observatory', *Country Life*, 11 June 1981.
6 Harris, pp. 83–4.
7 Royal Archives, Windsor Castle, Queen Charlotte to Prince Augustus, 13 June 1792.
8 W. H. Pyne, *Royal Residences*, I (1819), pp. 1–21.
9 *King's Works*, VI, pp. 373–9.
10 Royal Library, Windsor Castle, 1B 4a, Nathaniel Kent's Journal, 3 vols (MS).
11 Philip Howard, *Royal Palaces* (1970), p. 71.
12 Victoria & Albert Museum, A189, James Wyatt's plans for Kew; *King's Works*, VI, pp. 356–8.

IX. GEORGE IV

1 Clifford Musgrave, *Brighton Pavilion* (1951), p. 38.
2 *Survey of London*, XX, pp. 71–2.
3 Robert Adam, *Works in Architecture*, I (1778).
4 Horace Walpole to the Countess of Upper Ossory, 17 September, 1785.
5 Musgrave, *op. cit.*
6 Dorothy Stroud, *Henry Holland* (1966).
7 Thomas Sheraton, *Cabinet Maker and Upholsterer's Drawing Book* (1793), XXXI & XXXII.
8 W. H. Pyne, *Royal Residences*, III (1819), pp. 11–84. Pyne's original watercolours are preserved in the Royal Library at Windsor.
9 Farington, 3 May 1806.
10 Pyne, *op. cit.*, P.R.O. Works 5/94; Royal Archives 25340.
11 Musgrave, p. 60.
12 *Ibid*, p. 27.
13 Dorothy Stroud, *Humphrey Repton*, (1962), p. 138.
14 *Ibid*; Repton's designs for Brighton Pavilion are in the Royal Library at Windsor.
15 Musgrave, *op. cit.*
16 Musgrave, p. 38.
17 John Summerson, *The Life and Work of John Nash* (1980), pp. 94–5.
18 P.R.O., Works 1/11.
19 P.R.O., Works 1/12, pp. 406–7.
20 B.M., Add MS 38760, f 206.
21 *King's Works*, VI, p. 265.
22 *Ibid*, pp. 280–1.
23 Soane Museum correspondence 2, xii, B.2, ff 1–4.

X. VICTORIA AND ALBERT

1 P.R.O., Works 37/7, p. 8; Victoria & Albert Museum 8738/13, Edward Blore's designs for the east front of Buckingham Palace; Hermione Hobhouse, *Thomas Cubitt* (1971), pp. 394–426.
2 Clifford Smith, *Buckingham Palace* (1931), p. 176.
3 Ludwig Grüner, *The Decoration of the Garden Pavilion . . . Buckingham Palace* (1846).

4 *The Letters of Queen Victoria*, eds Benson A. C. and Viscount Esher (1907). Queen Victoria to Leopold, King of the Belgiums, 20 March 1845.
5 Quoted in James Pope-Hennessy, *Queen Mary* (1959), p. 331.
6 *Letters of Queen Victoria*, 8 June 1846.
7 John Charlton, *Guidebook to Osborne House* (HMSO, 1955); *The Builder*, VI (1848), pp. 570–1.
8 *Letters of Queen Victoria*, 1844.
9 *The Greville Memoirs*, ed. H. Reeve (8 vols., 1874–87).
10 Edinburgh University Library, Rowand Anderson, Kinimouth Paul Coll., William Smith's designs for Balmoral Castle; J. C. Morton, *The Prince Consort's Farms* (1863), p. 45.
11 Tyler Whittle, *Victoria and Albert at Home* (1980), pp. 44–5.
12 Morton, pp. 75–107.
13 *Ibid*, pp. 66, 72, 136, 156.
14 John Betjeman and John Piper, *Murray's Berkshire Architectural Guide* (1949), p. 152.

SELECT BIBLIOGRAPHY

BEATTIE, J. M., *The English Court in the Reign of George I* (1967).

BRITTON, J. AND BRAYLEY, E. W., *The Ancient Palace of Westminster* (1836).

CHAMBERS, E. K., *The Elizabethan Stage* (1923).

CHAMBERS, SIR WILLIAM, *Plans, Elevations, Sections and Perspective Views of the Gardens and Buildings at Kew* (1763).

Collection of Ordinances and Regulations for the Government of the Royal Household made in reigns from King Edward II to King William and Queen Mary (Society of Antiquaries, 1790).

COLVIN, H. M., *Royal Buildings* (1968).

COLVIN, H. M., *Biographical Dictionary of British Architects 1600–1840* (1978).

COLVIN, H. M., ed., *History of the King's Works*, I, II, III, V, VI (1963) Vol. IV not yet published.

DENT, JOHN, *The Quest for Nonsuch* (1962, reprinted 1981).

DUNLOP, IAN, *Palaces and Progresses of Elizabeth I* (1962).

EYTON, E. W., *Court, Household and Itineraries of Henry II* (1878).

GRAEME, B., *Story of St James's Palace* (1929).

HARRIS, JOHN, etc., *The King's Arcadia* (1973).

HARRIS, JOHN, etc., *Buckingham Palace* (1968).

HIBBERT, CHRISTOPHER, *The Court at Windsor, A Domestic History* (1964).

HOWARD, PHILIP, *Royal Palaces* (1970).

LAW, ERNEST, *History of Hampton Court Palace*, 3 vols. (1885–91).

LETHABY, W. R., 'The Palace of Westminster in the Eleventh and Twelfth Centuries', *Archaeologia*, IX (1906).

MALFATTI, C. V., *Two Italian Accounts of Tudor England* (1953).

MATTHEW, G., *Court of Richard II* (1968).

MORSHEAD, SIR OWEN, *Windsor Castle* (1957).

MORSHEAD, SIR OWEN, *George IV and Royal Lodge* (1965).

MURRAY-BAILLIE, HUGH, 'Etiquette and the Planning of the State Apartments in Baroque Palaces', *Archaeologia*, CI (1967).

MUSGRAVE, CLIFFORD, *Brighton Pavilion* (1951).

MYERS, A. R., *Household of Edward IV* (1959).

NICHOLS, J., *Progresses and Public Processions of Queen Elizabeth I*, 3 vols. (1923).

OPPÉ, E. A., *English Drawings at Windsor Castle* (1956).

PEVSNER, N., *Buildings of England* (1951).

PYNE, W. H., *Royal Residences*, 3 vols. (1819).

RYE, W. B., *England as seen by Foreigners* (1865).

ST JOHN HOPE, W. H., *Windsor Castle, an Architectural History*, 2 vols. (1913).

SALZMAN, L. F., *Building in England down to 1540* (1952).

SEDGWICK, ROMNEY, ed., *Lord Hervey, Some Materials for the Memoirs of the Reign of George II* (1931).

SHEPPARD, E., *Memorials of St James's Palace*, 2 vols. (1894).

SMITH, H. CLIFFORD, *Buckingham Palace* (1931).

STRONG, R. AND ORGEL, S., *Inigo Jones, The Theatre of the Stuart Court* (1973).

SUMMERSON, SIR JOHN, *Architecture in Britain 1530–1830*,

Survey of London, XIII (1930), XIV (1931) Whitehall.

TOUT, T. F., *Chapters in the History of Medieval England*, II (1920).

TOUT, T. F., 'Beginnings of a Modern Capital', *Collected Papers*, III (Manchester, 1934).

Vetusta Monumenta, VI (1842), Westminster.

WHITAKER-WILSON, C., *Whitehall Palace* (1934).

WHITTLE, TYLER, *Albert and Victoria at Home* (1980).

WOLFFE, B., *Royal Demesne* (1971).

Wren Society Publications 20 vols. (1924–43) especially VII, 'Royal Palaces of Winchester, Whitehall, Kensington and St James's'.

INDEX

Numbers in italics refer to black-and-white illustrations